GARDENS OF
REMEMBRANCE

GARDENS OF REMEMBRANCE

Thomas McCarthy

New Island Books/Dublin

Gardens of Remembrance
First published 1998 by
New Island Books
2 Brookside
Dundrum Road
Dublin 14
Ireland

British Library Cataloguing in Publication Data
A catalogue record for this book is available from the British Library

ISBN 1 874597 66 9

New Island Books receives financial assistance from The Arts Council (An Chomhairle Ealaíon), Dublin, Ireland.

Cover image: *Portrait of My Son, Shane* by Joan Jameson
Cover design: Slick Fish Design
Typesetting: New Island Books
Printed by in the Republic of Ireland by Colour Books, Dublin

ACKNOWLEDGEMENTS

Thanks especially to Catherine.

The author gratefully acknowledges the support of the *Arts Council of Ireland*, *The Irish American Cultural Institute* and *The American-Irish Foundation* (now *The Ireland Funds)* for generous support in the past. Thanks to *The Munster Literature Centre*, especially Mary Johnson.

Thanks, also, to three great friends in Minnesota: Thomas Dillon Redshaw, John Bernstein and Cindy Syme.

To the editors of various journals who accepted these essays and reviews, some in totally different form, grateful acknowledgement is made: *The Examiner, The Irish Times, Connaught Tribune, The Sunday Tribune, Stet, The Irish Review, New Hibernia Review, Eire Ireland, Poetry Ireland Review, Waterford Review.*

Finally, thanks to the Jameson family of Tourin, Co Waterford for permission to use the cover painting by Joan Jameson.

for
Anthony Cronin and Patrick Galvin

CONTENTS

PART ONE

Five Summer Afternoons

Memory, Childhood and the Party

There are days when I long for someone blind to come back again to reimpose order upon my life. From my deepest childhood I recall a blind and handsome old woman shuffling across an old-fashioned kitchen, from the dresser with its three rows of blue and brown willow-pattern plates to the wood and turf fire with its highly polished bellows-wheel. The woman was my paternal grandmother, one of the Brays of Mount Melleray. Everyone called her Nan-Nan. She had been born on the 26th of June 1888 into a family of small farmers, tradesmen and workers at the famous Cistercian Abbey. Her family was always proud of its closeness to the Cistercian community, its loving familiarity with monks who were carpenters and farmers, and priests who were bee-keepers and poultry-men as well as philosophers.

People who are born and reared in the environment of Mount Melleray are special and superior. They have grown up on first-name terms with men who are holy, men who filled the bleak upland of my part of West Waterford with the significance of meditated things. There was an aura about Nan-Nan Bray that was rich and secure. In her background were all the names of the Mount Melleray district, the Lyons, Condons, Coffeys, Carrolls and O'Donnells; all the Patricks, Daniels, Dominicks, Johannas and Brigids that stretch from the baptism of her father in December of 1852 to the cousins listening to her radio on Munster Final day of 1959.

Then my memories of her begin. Adults seemed drawn to her for gossip and advice. Her kitchen was as busy as a saddler's shop, full of country people coming to check her pigs, listen to her radio, eat her potatoes or the beautiful soft bread from Barron's Bakery covered with Ballinamult butter. My own mother used to say, ruefully, that her kitchen was like the Mount Melleray Bread-Bin that never ran out during the Great Famine.

I am not sure of the circumstances that led me into the arms of my grandmother. People say I was sent to live with her because I was sensible and very useful with my hands. My uncle also lived with her. A typical Irish bachelor, he was by turns innocent and mischievous, feckless and kind. He was very handsome, and considered himself a star with women. But he spent his days avoiding serious attachments.

My grandmother, though, sought out and held attachments with emotional ferocity. Hence, the sideboard full of mementoes, tiny lustreware coffee cups, luminous plastic Blessed Virgins, windowsills and garden steps covered with geraniums. An ornament or a geranium was always a gift from someone, or a reminder of someone far away, a brother at Roscrea or a nun in a Belfast convent. It was through my grandmother that I learned the power of personal attachments as well as the astonishing breadth of kinship and interdependence of country people. Interestingly, I was sent to live with my grandmother at precisely that point in time when my own mother's influence began to wane among my father's family. The politics of families fascinates me. It is the first politics we learn to abide by and survive. There was something between my mother and my grandmother, some wordless falling-out that happens so often in Irish families. It was a mystery to me. My grandmother, unbraiding the long grey hair in her nightly ritual while the kettle boiled for our ceramic hot-water bottles, spoke quietly of her disappointment in my father. He had been her brightest child, the one she had hoped would leap into definite respectability. Instead, he had turned into a dismal, depressed failure.

I didn't agree with her sentiments, but I maintained a respectful silence. I was eight years old, incredibly in tune with adult conversations. I knew how things were and I could carry a burden to bed on my own, especially after eating the Lincoln Creams and filling the water bottles that had the colour and texture of salt cellars. My bond with this dignified, elderly Bray, who had buried two husbands, was deep and powerful. I see patterns of attachment through my adolescence and into adulthood that repeat the first love I had for Nan-Nan. The grace and ease of the elderly is something that gives me great joy, and I find it difficult to trust anyone under the age of seventy.

My uncle was a member of the Labour Party. He always stood with Willie O'Donoghue behind the table at the Church gates during the Annual Collection for the Labour Party. He drank with Labour buddies in Walsh's Hotel. My grandmother didn't have much time for him. The politics she understood was the politics of the Party. As DeValera's eyesight diminished he rose in her estimation, until, in total blindness, he attained the status of a God. The Mount Melleray people who flocked to her kitchen on a Fair Day in Cappoquin were nearly all Fianna Fáil supporters. No questions asked. Fine Gael was mainly supported by farmer-blow-ins who got fine Blackwater valley farms from the Land Commission.That was a detail never lost on the small-holders of Mount Melleray, Scrahan and Crow Hill.

When I was a very young child my own father was never involved in Fianna Fáil. He was too troubled, poor and depressed to be involved in anything except getting through another terrible day. It was John Fraher, a neighbour, who persuaded my father and mother to join Fianna Fáil. By then I was already involved in the Party, going about not my father's business, but my grandmother's. But that was a few years down the road. At the moment of childhood remembered now, some night in 1962 or 1963, my grandmother combs out her extraordinary grey hair in a gesture of blind refinement. Something like the perfect gesture of a successful poem. DeValera is somewhere in the wings, in the faded pages of *The Irish Press*, or *The Cork Examiner* sent down by a neighbour, Mrs. Flanagan. But my grandmother combs out the days and years. She wears the ubiquitous blue check apron and black cardigan of an Irish countrywoman, or any European peasant woman from Bohemia to Barrack Street, Cappoquin.

It was her world that mattered. She was the Matriarch and I was the most tolerated one. When I turned in my secure bed, markedly different with its hard bolster and double white sheets from the flimsy sheets of my father's house, I thought of her landscape only, her neighbours, my cousins. As children we adhere to the social atmosphere of those we love. My grandmother's world extended down the stairs, past Jip the indifferent terrier, out the backyard with its brilliant white-washed walls, up the steps to a vegetable garden crammed with potatoes, onions and cabbage, onto the long piggery that was built against the estate wall of Sir Richard Keane's domain.

But, first, on the way to that vast garden, past the heavily scented common lilac, *Syringa Vulgaris*, you had to stop to check the geraniums for water. In late May, the geraniums, brilliant double reds, scented, a hundred of them at least, were at their most promising. By late May, Nan-Nan would know which plants had survived the winter. Dead geraniums would be moved to the back of a dense forest of bloom, into a dark corner to await the production of new slips. The vegetable garden itself was criss-crossed by a network of canals, deep channels that were filled with slurry from the piggery. That slurry produced flowery spuds and the darkest green cabbage you ever ate, a deadly bowel-scrubber. Vegetables, lilac and geraniums and a few luscious pink rambler roses that burst into bloom across the corrugated red roof of her timber shed, those were the things grown and cared for.

Lying awake at night, dreaming immense dreams of a child, I would sometimes be startled into consciousness by my uncle slamming the hall door after the pub. I would worry for the crockery left on the table, the lustreware cups from Rome that we had taken down to dust and polish. Would he stumble, would he break them? He never did. Not one thing was ever broken in that house. Because of her blindness, everyone moved as if they couldn't see very well. In this way everything was saved.

Awake in bed I used to think of all the things she had. Instead of counting sheep, I'd think of a cupboard and list all the unused things in that cupboard. Sometimes I'd think of a press falling over and imagine all the breakables that might be broken. I used to contrast the house of my father, with its Quaker austerity and lack of things, with Nan-Nan's home that was like a warehouse of souvenirs. For example, her bedroom that looked out over the geranium-scented yard was an obstacle course of hanging fabrics and metal-lined chests. From one long rail hung a series of body-length transparent covers that contained woollen and tweed coats, and silk blouses: wool grown knobbly with age and silk or linen yellowed with age and lack of use. In what previous life had she made use of these clothes? In my childhood she never wore anything except the sober dress of an Irish widow. Once or twice I succeeded in lifting the heavy lid of a zinc-lined trunk: full of linens. What were these things doing in her house? Had she kept them since she was first married in the years after the First World War?

In the sitting-room, always called 'the back-room', there were two possessions that filled me with awe. The first was an Edwardian stereoscope, complete with double-slides of faraway places, Continental gardens, a Venetian canal scene, St Peter's Square in Rome. I spent long winter evenings and wet summer days gazing at these images. At night I dreamed of Rome. I thought it must be a place like Mount Melleray Abbey, full of gifted Cistercians who kept silent and cared for honey-bees. The other possession that caught my fancy was a small blue wind-up gramophone: something that I couldn't play without letting the whole house in on the secret. There was a stack of HMV 78s, mainly of Big Band music, Thirties waltzes, fox-trots, even one or two tangos. When I placed the thick needle on the heavy black disk and pumped like mad, the house filled with music, sending Jip howling from his basket under the stairs. My grandmother laughed, the deep chair creaking with her laughter.

I would turn in bed, alone in the upstairs rooms with an old woman, absolutely contented. The pride she had in herself, in her appearance and her household, was a force that ran through my veins. I participated in her pride every Sunday and on the mornings of a Fair Day in Cappoquin. Cousins who came in for breakfast or to listen to a hurling match on the radio had to wait for me to find the extra cups, the spare knives, the cream jug, the egg beater. I was Nan-Nan's deputy, the keeper of her possessions. There was about her a certain style, a daintiness of movement or gesture. I used to think it had something to do with blindness. My grandmother had a daintiness that was unusual, perhaps accentuated and in some way codified by that blindness. 'Daintiness' meant putting on airs, a thing frowned upon by simple people – yet acknowledged in an envious way.

I think it must be a genetic thing, a strange code of gentility that survives without interrogation, like linen and silk in a wooden trunk. Fifteen years after my grandmother's death I was taking a piece of cake from a plate in the kitchen of a daughter of an old neighbour of my grandmother's from Mount Melleray: "Sure, will you take the ting in yer hand! Honest to God!" she exclaimed, "You're as dainty as the old

Melleray Brays." When I asked her what she meant, she told me precisely what I knew. I was as fastidious as a curate who has risen from a poor family, putting on airs, acting above myself. Some genetic sport that controlled my grandmother's life of blindness completely had rubbed off slightly upon me. It is a trait that throws out an elaborate protective mechanism.

"You are as dainty as your grandmother."

Our evenings together filled the longest stretch of my childhood. She would tell stories, about life on a small farm, the War of Independence, the cross-roads dances and the people who played Forty-Five while Indian meal boiled on the open fire. Once she recalled the large slices of gingerbread that she and her brothers took to the neighbourhood school at the gates of Mount Melleray. The gingerbread set them apart. She said she didn't give a damn.

"Thomas, throw water on the fire. We don't want the house to burn down."

Down the long hair would come, for the nightly ritual. Being beautiful takes concentration and care. Being blind since her early twenties, she must have felt beautiful until the day of her death. Twice widowed – I was called after her first husband, Thomas McCarthy of Knockanore who'd married her in Cappoquin Church in February 1918 – every night she became a young woman again, a spoilt beauty in the everlasting house of memory.

When I think of her I confuse her voice with that of the elderly DeValera. Dev spoke with her voice, a soft, delicate Deise-like Clare voice. Within his voice was the tremble of the new curate. I often played a seventy-eight record with his voice that was stored in a brown cardboard folder. She would hear the record playing and shout "Turn it up, make it louder". I would be sitting in the back room and she would be sitting in the kitchen by the fire. From where I sat on the highly polished linoleum I could see the back of her head, her silver hair and her quite delicate hand twitching on the arm-rest. We would listen together to the voice of Dev, his lilting, pining lament for the martyred Kevin Barry.

Years later when DeValera died I heard the same voice played on the radio. My grandmother had been dead six or seven years and everything seemed to have been scattered. One day in 1969 my Uncle Mick called me out of the classroom in St Anne's, Cappoquin, to tell me that Nan-Nan had died. The day she died the past was closed over my childhood and a tin box marked 'Childhood' was sealed. Feelings and dreams that had endlessly expanded in her household were consigned to dust. And years after that, when I was a student at UCC, I returned to her in a simple poem:

> In her blindness
> the house became
> a tapestry of touch.
> The jagged end of a dresser
> became a signpost
> to the back-door,
>
> bread crumbs crunching
> under her feet told
> her when to sweep
> the kitchen floor.

('Her Blindness')

It was her soft voice, hardly ever raised in anger, that I connected with my first Fianna Fáil world. It was a world of the elderly, the world of those who reminisce, the world of small shopkeepers and modest hope. The kind of people who came into my grandmother's kitchen, Tom Poole and Mrs Nagle, the Melleray Brays, Mrs Colbert of Colbert's shop, a cousin of Nan-Nan's, the stray cousins who lingered until a full meal was served, people from Aherne's shop and Frahers' newsagents – all were hard-working, decent Fianna Fáil folk. The green train of the Great Southern and Western Railways that steamed out of Cappoquin at four in the afternoon carried passengers out of the unchanging landscape of the Party. My grandmother sighed to hear the train go, clearly heard and felt as it moved beneath the embankment below McCarthy's Desmond Cinema.

'The bank' was what we called that landscaped glen with two streams. It was a childhood territory of watercress and sticklebacks or cobleens, minnows that were trapped in pools and hunted with jam-jars. It is true that in boyhood there's no time frame. Some people think that this notion is a poet's invention, a product of Wordsworth's or Heaney's imagination. Instead it is a quality of being that a child falls into naturally, a quality that the middle-aged can only remember. There were days down the bank that my cousin John and I spent in such complete concentration that the time passed could have been ten minutes or five hours.

In this way memory becomes as unreliable as childhood. The hearth of my past is my grandmother's world. The strings of discipline that bound me to a place were held by someone who was blind. My parents assumed, or wanted to assume, that all of my childhood was spent in Nan-Nan's kitchen, doing my homework and helping out. My grandmother's place was only a centre from where I roamed when all the chores were done. Childhood was busy, but its business grew out of an uninterrupted solitude. This is why to this day I exhibit many of the vanities and solitary habits of an only child. Nowadays my need to be alone is less urgent, but when I was a child and a teenager my failure to be left alone could make me physically ill. It is ironic, then, that I was drawn out of my childhood when I grasped at the coat-tails of some of the elderly cousins and neighbours who were inside Fianna Fáil. Involvement in politics is born out of some exaggerated personal need. Politics is built upon aspirations and hopes. At around the age of twelve I left my grandmother's house and went back to live permanently with my parents. Theirs was an entirely different place, a three-bedroomed terraced house with too many children in the neighbourhood and too many dogs barking everywhere.

Compared to the marvellous excess of Nan-Nan's home, there was too little of everything now to satisfy my highly developed need for choice. I complained bitterly and grew to despise my father. I didn't hate the man. In fact I loved him, as my brothers and sister loved him, for his intelligence, his days of supreme good humour and his political cynicism. Children are never too young to enjoy the full force of a really vicious political comment. My father had such a highly developed cynicism that it clashed violently with the anecdotal goodness of politics I had taken from years in my grandmother's house. It wasn't until I went to UCC and listened to cynical comments by witty professors that I found men who could compete with my father. Both of my parents supported Fianna Fáil, despite my mother's Dungarvan Republican heritage and my father's adoration of Noel Browne. Browne was the great victim in my father's eyes, and through the failure of his Mother and Child Scheme one could see all the powerful and evil forces at work against the poor.

For my parents, DeValera was already a jaded figure. He shuffled across the TV screen, vestigial and blind. When I was twelve and thirteen Lemass and Haughey were the big fish, the ones to reckon with. Older people, though, still had their standards, or should I say prejudices. I remember during the Presidential election of 1966 getting a clatter across the face from an elderly neighbour because I told her (foolishly) that I'd written an essay on Tom O Higgins as my favourite candidate.

"You are one stupid child," she said after checking that her assault really had hurt.

"What has dat fella Higgins done for you or for anyone belongin' to ya?"

It was a comment I remembered as I considered voting for Garret FitzGerald's candidates in the mid-Eighties. Nothing like physical pain to drive home a political tradition. Perhaps it was the fear of another (metaphorical) slap in the face that drove me to Paris in the late eighties:

> *Two referenda lost, we took the inner seats*
> *and flew to Paris through wind and sleet.*

> * * *

> *Should we go now, to spread the gospel*
> *of poems, ten Metro tickets surviving*
> *in your purse. For Garret Parnell is dead.*

('Seven Winters in Paris')

It is the idea of France that Irish people are bred to believe in: France, the father of all republics and the mother of all fairplay. Not that France and my small hometown on the Blackwater were always far apart. In fact, in the post-Famine era it was the electricity of French ideas that determined a good deal of Cappoquin history and social development. The Paris Revolution of 1848 inspired a group of Young Irelanders to attack Government establishments in Ireland. They were defeated in the usual debacle, but a few survived and fled to fight another day. In September of 1849 a group of Young Ireland socialists returned and attacked Cappoquin Barracks, led by the local journalist Joseph Brennan. A man was killed on each side. Most of the leaders escaped to America, but eleven Young Irelanders were transported to Bermuda and Tasmania.

This revolutionary act led to the posting of a garrison regiment in my hometown, and this in turn led to the establishment of the Convent of Mercy to oversee the morals of local women who might be tempted to 'go with soldiers'.

The Cappoquin of my childhood, the teeming market-town of the Party, had changed very little from the heady political days of the 1850s. Young men and women crowded the streets, pouring out of The Cappoquin Bacon Factory and O'Connor's Chickens to change their cheques in Maurice Kelleher's or James Russell's shops. It was the era of the blue-collar hero. Education was laughed at. Jobs were easy to come by, especially if you had a friend or lover already working in 'the Factory' or O'Connor's. The elite of my hometown were not the doctors or teachers, but the van-driver salesmen like Willie Moore and Jim Landers who knew every shopkeeper and hurler from Kenmare to Kells.

Between 1964 and 1972 (when I left Cappoquin to go to College) the footpaths, Co-Op Stores, churchyard, Boathouse Ballroom, 'Bank' walk and town park seemed alive with the laughter of the very young. In this atmosphere the Party thrived. The Labour Party, under the steady gaze of Willie O'Donoghue, seemed to thrive as well.

At around that time, David Thornley wrote a series of perceptive articles on Irish political parties for *The Irish Times*. He wrote about Lemass's legacy, Fianna Fáil:

> The ossification of time had almost turned the Party into a federation of introverted local autonomies ... Since 1959 Mr Lemass has worked wonders with this material. He has cemented the loyalties while refurbishing the image. Thirty years ago this was a Party of republicanism, language revival, economic protection: today it is a Party of realism, talks with Captain O'Neill, growth, planning, free trade. The leadership still cannot wholly exert its will upon the constituency organisations. But it has shifted many of the

old castes and brought in young men who are not merely clever but tough.

(*Irish Times*, April 1, 1965)

In the late Sixties in Cappoquin, walking the footpath in Barrack Street, Allen Street or Main Street with Ned Lonergan or Councillor Ahern or Quirke, greeting people to the sound of the Factory siren, the Co-Op steam valves or the constant hammering in Sargent's Garage, it was easy to believe that history might never be interrogated again. It was the first and last time in Irish life when people seemed entirely absorbed in the present. The past belonged to the elderly or those who didn't have a car, or a friend with a car, who'd drive them to Redbarn or Clonea. What is so amazing now is that it took so long for Ulster to happen to us. There wasn't even one cloud on the horizon of public life, certainly no cloud that Gay Byrne or Angela MacNamara couldn't have sorted out by the week's end. As my Uncle Mick used to love saying, "Everything is sorted now".

Until Ulster happened it seemed that nothing could go wrong. No theory would be tested and no generalisation brought under scrutiny. For a few brief years everything went the way of the Party. The Lemass era slipped quietly into the Lynch era. I remember shaking hands with Lynch at the Irish College in Ballingeary in the summer of 1967. He was such a 'dacent' Corkman, even Waterford people liked him. He epitomised the tepid waters of Irish politics in the late Sixties.

The dorm at the Irish college was full of earnest Fianna Fáil youths on GAA Gaeltacht scholarships. Perhaps years later the same youths (by then anorak-wearing men of means) would use the phrases handed out on phrase cards by Party officials at a National Conference: *Nach raibh oraid an Taoisigh go hiontach* (Wasn't the Taoiseach's speech great!) or *Ta an halla ag lionadh go tapaidh* (The hall is filling up quickly). Such things, such a repetition of clichés until even feelings are standardised, are deeply offensive to the educated reader. But in a Catholic culture where even personal prayer is standardised, the use of clichés can hardly be a surprise. At some point in every young Fianna Fáil activist's life the future seems to hold nothing but *'ceol, canadh agus rince'*. The words for such a feeling of well-being needn't be personal at all, for such feelings come from crowds and power.

When I was eighteen I tried to write a play about the Party: that very specific part in the Lismore Electoral Area. Labour Parties and other Socialist parties always produce their writers, I thought, so why couldn't the experience of Fianna Fáil, which is so pre-literate, so lacking in re-imagination, produce its own signature in writing? It was a foolish and fatal act on my part. I lost friends in poetry who were socialists, who couldn't stand this obsession of mine with 'the Party'. It was as if I couldn't fully withdraw from its atmosphere. Many respectable people (and quite rational people, in other ways) see Fianna Fáil as a kind of religious cult; a thing to prevent one's children from getting into. This is totally unfair, of course. But there's no point in presenting the argument because the intellectual odds are stacked so heavily against one.

I remember a history teacher at school taking me aside after class one day because my name had appeared in the *Dungarvan Leader* as Treasurer of the local *Cumann*. "What are you doing with that lot?" the teacher asked. "Your whole life is ahead of you. You could be something." I didn't know what to say. Was this person telling me that the likes of Ned Lonergan, Tom Lincoln, or John Fraher were unsavoury people? I just didn't know what to do. My father, of course, had fallen out with Fianna Fáil types. He had read something about Noel Browne and he was away on a high horse about the rich scoundrel Haughey, the bore deValera, the foolish anti-worker Minister Smith.

Literature comes from personalised material. One writes in order to explain oneself personally, completely. The dialogue of politics is always polemical, one-sided, argumentative whereas the work of poetry feeds upon ambiguity; it presents both the argument and its rebuttal. A poem doesn't work unless it first worked at the personal level of the poet. I couldn't handle the technical difficulty of drama: I didn't know enough about life. That was for sure. But I knew about canvassing on Melleray Road. So I wrote about that:

Local Election

The wet latch breaks open, a rusty gate
swings wide. New shoes push year-old weeds aside.
Dead stalks rot there by the hedge where spring died.
A rhododendron layers at snail's rate.
The Virgin's blue in the window keeps faith
inside green walls. The paint peels from the knob
as we knock. The kettle-crash on the hob
shows surprise. A knife sings along a plate.
Our candidate is practically you:
his village past, hens in potato rows,
absentee Lords and haunted Christmas snow.
And we were shocked by television too!
A successful canvas? God only knows
as we check our list. Six homes to go.

I can detect Kavanagh, and Larkin's tone in 'Our candidate is practically you'. But it was a beginning. It was where the Party began again for me; an imaginary place where all kinds of tension, personal and political, could be played out. Even then I thought if I could get the details right the politics would take care of itself. This is how politics works anyway.

Even today I find that there are critics who want to rescue me from this material. This *petit-bourgeois* world of domestic

Irish politics is seen as sterile, a cul-de-sac. I am fully aware poetry can never come from crowds and power. It comes from that part of the spirit that flees from power. It is important not to get confused about this matter. There are basic principles of art at stake when poets become too comfortable with crowded smoke-filled committee rooms. Poetry rages against the kind of values that win over the crowd. In recent years there has been a growth of performance poetry and an increasing market for people who are better performers than poets. The same has always been true in politics. I have seen it happen personally, at a local and national level. In public life there are always figures who are better politicians than leaders. But they add nothing to the life of a country, any more than a dramatic second-rate poet adds to the life of literature. The sincerity of a poetry reading comes directly from the sincerity of the poet. There is a presentation of values that the audience shares. Nobody is fooled and nobody is betrayed. On the contrary, something like adult life is delineated and recognised.

At the present time in Ireland poets and poetry have a very high profile. It reminds me of the days in Fianna Fáil, those heady days after the massive swing of 1977, when Party members felt immortal. What a disaster that was for all of us! Politics is different from poetry in many ways, but most emphatically in that perception about the nature of power. The good poets will always be read. They don't require elocution lessons, they certainly don't require the treachery of added drama. The text will speak. Like a flawless paragraph of leadership. The minute the crowd rises, the poet's head should be turned elsewhere.

Poetry, then, is more like memory than power. Only the truly innocent think it is power in the world's sense. It certainly is not. But it is like childhood, and it connects with the individual childhood of the reader. It is that space in a back-room where a phonograph is playing. Every adulthood has those beginnings. Poetry is one of the presences that emerges from the private ether. Beware of public men bearing poems. The poem is rarely full of political power. It is rather like the Irish phrase on a card at a Party conference, or the prayer-cards that old people carry. No politician should use a poet in order to speak with God.

Then again, I am prejudiced because I am a loner. I was in the Party because of an accident of geography and a circumstance of childhood. Ultimately, politics can only be a subject-matter, a material on the way to poems. The companionship offered by politics is such a drug that writers can hardly survive it. The best thing for a poet to do is to see all political involvement as a kind of childhood. In that way power is seen for what it is, something to be put away in exchange for adult things. In my own case the adult thing is the world created by books. Now, in my own life, the Party itself has become a thing of remembrance, something that I have walked beyond in a dual search for adulthood and poetry. I cannnot detach it from my earlier image: an elegant old woman, Nan-Nan Bray, hesitating for one moment beside the dresser in a silent, 1960s kitchen.

A Short Walk in the Snow

There is a photograph of Glenshelane Wood near Cappoquin that my brother Michael took nearly twenty years ago. It is a beautiful image, both haunting and intriguing: a snow-covered woodland road, well defined by a canopy of frozen trees, that ebbs away from the cold blue foreground. There is an incredible sense of stillness: that dead calm of a blue cold winter morning in the woods when the world is emptied of life.

My brother has captured the moment perfectly. Twenty years ago all our lives were in a winterish repose. Our mother had just died and our father was not long dead; both parents taken from us suddenly, catastrophically, at the age of fifty-five: too young for fathers and mothers to die. They died just after they'd emerged from the long hard passage of working-class Ireland towards the light of the Seventies. The unfairness of it all cut a deep and permanent trench in my personality. Michael's photograph of snow captures the essence of our broken family at that moment in time. When that photograph was taken we all felt truly alone in the world:

> *It is an image of irreversible loss,*
> *This hole in my father's grave that needs*
> *Continuous filling. Monthly now, my*
> *Uncle comes to shovel a heap of earth*
> *From the spare mound. Tear-filled, he*
> *Compensates the collapse of his brother's*
> *Frame . . . .*

('Hole, Snow')

Grief had taken hold of me like a coma. I could only read books about grief and lost fathers. The flowers of grief that were found in books became a kind of feast for me, a continuing last supper. I didn't realise it then, but I was given the enormous privilege of being left alone with my grief. Nobody interrupted me. Nowadays we crowd around the bereaved, fearful that they are afraid of the silence of the beloved they've lost. It is our own helplessness that we are afraid of, that nagging sense of being useless to the ones we love.

Nothing will ever replace the dead who have gone from us. There is no point in looking for a replacement, as if a dog or a cat had just died, because the feeling of grief is a new thing in our lives. It is death that creates a new relationship between ourselves and the one who has gone away. We can never touch them again, to embrace or injure them, for the relationship will be carried on through a kind of psychic correspondence.

In the late Seventies, a sudden wintertime that followed the summers of 1975–76, I dreamt my way out of grief. I continued to garden at Glenshelane House with Denis FitzGerald, who had lost his brother, the writer, Brian FitzGerald, around the same time. Denis was a wonderful stabilising influence just at that moment, but also a quiet and creative friend. I took long walks through the woods on my own or took long train journeys on my own, stopping now and again to write letters to old friends from College. The train journeys I took had a special other-worldly quality. Ironically, at times of great stress, travel and movement can offer a peculiarly personal kind of stillness. While I travelled and gardened I read Edmund Gosse's *Father and Son*, di Lampedusa's *Places of My Infancy*, as well as Gide's *If It Die* and Ó Ríordáin's 'Adhlacadh mo Mháthair' over and over again. There is something profoundly bookish about the death of parents. My wish for anyone bereaved is that they would find the book appropriate to their own individual sadness.

The snows then that fell in West Waterford, especially the snows of the Knockmealdowns, the Melleray and Newcastle roads and Glenshelane Wood, seemed a proper shroud that had fallen upon my frosted life. I think the core of my adult personality was created in those months of my parents' loss, as I thought about all they had suffered in that utterly bleak and sterile interlude of mid-century Ireland. Their last few years were good ones at a personal level. As he grew older my father grew warmer and more affectionate. He seemed to stop being afraid of his own life. While my mother basked in those occasional late happy days, weeks even, of extremely good-humoured companionship, she still carried the full, financial burden of the family. In the end, only she could read the real situation. Socially, their circumstances were still terrible and she had to carry on alone.

My parents were very different in character, the one bookish, cynical, reclusive, the other outgoing, trusting, devout. But their backgrounds were very similar. They had been born poor, had married poor and died even poorer. But as usual in Irish marriages it was my mother who had to bear the brunt of reality:

> *I must have seen you crying often*
> *after a Friday morning deluge of bills;*
> *but it is your girl's infectious laugh*
> *that reaches here through the years.*

('Helena')

It is never possible to capture the full impact of grief. After they died I felt that I lived within an interior life only: like a spell in a coma. Snow is a good metaphor for it all, though, because snow contains within it some of the hidden things, the sleeping life of hopes. I see Glenshelane Wood especially as a place of snow-covered tracks. For a poet trees are sacred things, having that ancient connection with the Irish alphabet as well as the resonance of so many Mad Sweeney poems, the mythical and mystical wild man of the woods, and Kilcash, that warm Gaelic household that fell with its trees and its poets, in words so brilliantly translated by Frank O'Connor:

> *What shall we do for timber?*
> *The last of the woods is down.*
> *Kilcash and the house of its glory*
> *And the bells of the house are gone.*

When I was an adolescent in Cappoquin – incredibly busy with school and demanding part-time jobs, early morning milk-rounds and weekend gardening – I escaped into Glenshelane Wood regularly. It was a magic place in a steep valley, with its bee-hives owned by the Lonergan brothers, old Mass-paths and a decaying tower-house supposedly built during the disturbances of 1848. It was the place of my adolescence, a canopied space where a teenager could go on long flights of imagination:

> *I watch the minutes passing away:*
> *the minutes are like bark of olearia*
> *blowing along the grass after a storm,*
> *each bark a negative of your dead face.*

('Helena')

The above lines were written some years after my mother's death. They are part of a lucky-bag of quatrains called 'Helena' – Helena, the pet-name my father used to tease my mother with. Her name was Ellen, her sisters and friends called her

Nellie. But the way my father used that name, Helena, intrigued me. It was meant to have Napoleonic overtones. It conveyed exile and loss of status. My father was a wise man, though a poor husband and provider. He walked the same woods as I did. In walking through that photograph of snow I was retracing a path that he and his brothers had walked many times. In the post-war years after he'd left the Army he worked with his brothers cutting and planting trees in Glenshelane:

> *Sometimes I return to where he belonged,*
> *to his most real world of felled trees*
> *and timber bridges;*
> *and I find, where*
> *time has had time to play,*
> *his first dimly-lit woodlander's hut*
> *covered by time's macramé*
> *of loosened ropes and beams.*

('In Memory of My Father')

When I was a child Glenshelane Wood was peppered with dimly-lit woodlanders' huts, quickly assembled boxes of recycled timber that were used for storing forestry equipment and providing bolt-holes of shelter during sudden downpours. In 1977 and again in 1979 we were drenched by the sudden downpour of our parents' deaths. Nothing in our lives together had prepared us for the loss of parents. I remember few moments of repose because my childhood was so busy. My brother, Michael, and my sister, Mary, who has an especially deep memory of things, do remember moments of repose as well as days of crisis.

It was difficult at that time to realise what was lost. Two parents who were really loved, one hard-working and humble, the other an impractical dreamer and full of misplaced snobbery. My relationship with my mother was one of continuous admiration and protectiveness. As a child I never ceased to want better things for her. Even as a child I believed that my father had a self-destructive gene, an inheritance that made him turn away from life and every tension of life that mattered: friendship, sport, working days and pub life. I have inherited a good deal of his desperate inertia. But my mother was made of finer stuff, energetic, brave, trusting, hopeful, loving human contacts.

Despite every misery that she suffered in Cappoquin she retained a strong sense of hope and a belief in the goodness of everything. My father, on the other hand, believed firmly in the hopelessness of his life and the hopelessness of our social situation in that small busy town by the Blackwater. He was an intelligent man, indeed a man of exceptional intelligence. One thing he couldn't hide was his admiration for our performance at school. He was especially thrilled by the mathematical gifts of his youngest son, Kevin, who went on to become an engineer and research scientist. He died too soon to see Kevin's fine academic achievements, but even he had to admit the unstoppable force of a really intelligent child. Our own efforts at college as well as my sister Mary's nurse's training in England stimulated my father to get back into his studies. Not that I was a great scholar. Quite the opposite. From the age of seventeen, when I acquired a real love of poetry, I drifted away from formal education. Exams never again held the same magic as a published poem.

Inspired by us, my father renewed his efforts to get a diploma in engineering. This followed his achievement in getting qualifications in accountancy. Books came out of the cupboards again in his final years. Books were always strewn around our home. My father was a reader; but a reader of non-fiction, geography and history, journalism and art and craft books. He lived so deeply inside his own head that he had no need for the corrective medicine of stories and novels (apart from a few Zane Greys and Irving Wallace). The presence of so many books did mark us off from our small town neighbours. I think it was due mainly to the presence of so many books that I grew up with the attitude of a more leisured class, rather than the working-class child that I really was.

Even today when I explain to people just how lacking in privilege my family was they don't quite believe me. It is books, really, that have marked my own character, as they saved my father from complete despair. One can escape through books. That is one part of their powerful virtue. The world forces us constantly, like a well-brought-up Gestalt therapist nagging us, pushing us, to accept our situation. Books remind us that we don't have to accept our situation in life. We need not. Why should we, if it doesn't suit our sensibility or our own private image of our noble selves? The books we own are like open train-tickets. Through them we have the option of going elsewhere.

From my father I inherited a love of reading, but more generally a love of displays of intelligence. The one thing that evoked an unambiguous, positive response from my father was some display of intelligence from us or from neighbours and friends.

Yet, in my childhood everything good that happened seemed to happen despite my father – or to spite him – whereas tragedies when they occurred fed his self-indulgent bleakness. I developed a habit very early on of editing everything that happened in my life when talking to him.

My grandmother and my mother encouraged me to edit everything I reported to him. To the end of her life I think my grandmother saw her grandchildren as unfair burdens that had been placed upon her own children. With the exception of my hard-working Uncle Michael who ran his shop, reared pigs and baked Christmas cakes for friends and neighbours despite constant illness, my grandmother reared a generation of weak and spoiled sons. On the other hand, her daughters were wonderful.

Perhaps I am too hard on my father. After all, as I take a short walk through the snow of Glenshelane Wood, I must remember the unpromising milieu that determined everything. The milieu of Cappoquin may have wrecked his mind. I admit as much. When he was very young my father had worked as a farm labourer, a soldier (during the Emergency), then a postman. He had finished his studies in book-keeping and accountancy when he suffered a nervous breakdown, brought on, we now know, by an earlier traffic accident.

Having suffered that breakdown, he never received any kind of adequate care. He became introverted, cantankerous, even suicidal. I remember one day arriving at my father's house (strange, I never called it 'home' when I was a boy – I saw my grandmother's house as 'home') only to be greeted with a stand-off between my demented mother and my father who was holding a blade in his hand and threatening to kill himself. "Give me the blade, for feck sake," I said angrily, "And cop on." His fit of suicidal rage was brought on probably because my mother refused to buy another expensive book or expensive tool for one of his hobbies.

For years we lived on the few hundred pounds in the bank, the proceeds of some settlement, then on my father's pension. I remember meeting my mother in Dinny Mescall's shop in the Square in Cappoquin one day. It must have been in May or June of 1966, because I know I was twelve years old. My mother had the look of death on her face. "There's only two hundred pounds left," she whispered to me as people from the country clamoured to be served by Dinny himself. "He wants another big accountancy book for an exam. What is he going to do with all this learning? He thinks there's hundreds and hundreds left." Now I can see what a terrible year that was for her, the beginning of the hardest decade of her life that was to end in her death from a stroke at the age of fifty-five. Lively and adored when she was a child in Dungarvan, she died exhausted.

I had argued with my father only the day before meeting my mother in Dinny Mescall's shop. Our argument wasn't about money or his duty to find a job, any job that he might condescend to try despite his multiple certificates and qualifications. My father and I had argued about plans to build a monument to the men of the 1916 Rising. He thought it was a waste of good money, whereas I thought that the dead should be honoured. At that stage my father was a member of Fianna Fáil, but a dissenting member. Dissension suited him. I was also in Fianna Fáil, but operating independently of my father and his Melleray cousins in the Party. I spent most of my spare time with John Fraher, who I admired greatly and with whom I served what could only be described as a constituency apprenticeship in the Lismore *Comhairle Dáil Ceanntar* of the Party. In fact, the practical events and catastrophes that I write about in my Party poems, from *The First Convention* of 1976 to *The Lost Province* of 1996 have more to do with John Fraher and my gallivanting around Cappoquin and Mount Melleray than with anything I ever experienced with my father. The 'father' in most cases is a manufactured figure, a kind of father, a metaphor. It is a bitter poetic truth in my life that the image of the father is always a metaphor of disappointment. But the sense of failure and failed promise is very accurate, and honestly reported, and has a great deal to do with my own experience as a disappointed son:

> *It breaks my heart to think of your failures,*
> *for you were not a bad man, just hopeless.*
> *The lost Party, those lethal social forces*
> *that broke your will broke others less poor.*

*Talent is a muscle that needs constant exercise
and Ireland was your disagreeable milieu.*

('Thinking of My Father in the Musée Picasso')

* * *

*Who will be responsible for my childhood
when the votes are counted? Where
will the blame fall?'*

('The Waiting Deputies')

* * *

*Why was my father powerless, and all my cousins?
What treachery did we commit against the Dáil?*

('The Lost Province of Alsace')

In circumstances of extremely limited opportunity, the situation of my father and others like him, men of no property with poor connections, there is only one rational option: emigration. As a child I could never forgive my father for refusing to go away, refusing to make use of those qualifications that others who left Ireland so sadly lacked. If he had gone away he would have soared. I have no doubt about it. He and all his brothers seemed rooted to the parish of Cappoquin. He did feel that the McCarthys went back a long way in Cappoquin, back beyond the time when Cappoquin was even a parish. He had McCarthy ancestors that went back to 1700 at least in the Cappoquin and Tourin area. But ancestry never put bread on the table.

That he didn't go away was a mark of his illness, his inertia. The ambience of Cappoquin disabled him and nullified his fine intelligent mind. For most of my childhood I was furious with him. My fury found sublimation in work. I had so many part-time jobs when I was a child that I ended each day exhausted. Exhausted, triumphant, raging: the sort of combination of feelings that one has in adulthood after writing a poem or a day of cutting turf. My father's own dissenting membership in the Party also had a profound effect on my adolescent self. I began to see a lack of political awareness, and any expression of boredom with politics, as a mark of illness in itself. As for emigration, I had no patience with my father. Better men before him had to go away; like Donal Foley of Ferrybank or Liam O'Flaherty of Aran. Ireland, like Italy or Portugal or Norway, always offered her sons that final poisoned chalice. For my father's generation exile could never be seen as failure, but an expression of frustrated strength and ambition. Something in my father made him terrified of success.

In circumstances like those of West Waterford in the late Forties, in the towns of Cappoquin, Lismore and Tallow, where the limited life-chances were already spoken for by the children of shop-keepers and minor officials, emigration was the only strong gesture available to the children of the poor. Ironically, membership of Fianna Fáil was no guarantee of a job. The only thing to be gained by membership was a warm greeting and the solidarity of numbers. Nothing in Fianna Fáil would prepare a child to do a good interview, certainly not a good Public Service interview. Privilege is a weird thing. In Ireland, as in most post-revolutionary states, it is well disguised.

The thing about Irish history, Fenian history and IRA history, is that it gave the holders of privilege and position a new vocabulary through which they might negotiate further life chances for themselves and their children. As Peadar O'Donnell noted, the numbers who flocked to the cause of the Free State Government when the Civil War broke out was mind-boggling. Their quick discovery of nationhood may have had something to do with the prospect of native clerical jobs. Many people today still wonder why Ireland's contribution to the British effort in the Great War was so completely forgotten. Surely it was forgotten because the native middle-class discovered a new source of pride and income, the Free State. The poor, on the other hand, who had shouldered the burden of the War of Independence as well as the burden of the Somme, found themselves once again behind barbed-wire fences. And still without significant work. What a tidy little concept 'security' is: it has kept significant numbers of intelligent poor children out of the reckoning for good jobs, both North and South, for well over sixty years.

I could never forgive my father for standing still. He was intelligent, aware of politics, even a member of a Fianna Fáil Cumann. Why didn't he go away? At some point in that terrible decade from 1948–1958 he must have seen that the game was up for him, and for men like him. The only door to success was the door of the ticket office on the platform of Cappoquin Station. But he was fatally attached to Cappoquin and his docile brothers and his indulgent mother.

At a time of grief so many things come together. Loneliness, rage, bitterness, cantankerous speech. When I grieved in the Seventies I was so aware of my rage with my father and his milieu. I pitied myself for being his son. There was no escaping him. He was attached to me as fathers are, like gangrenous appendages after a long trek in the snow.

But one cannot choose one's father. As I look at the photograph of snow falling in Glenshelane Wood I wonder what kind of father would I have chosen? For a writer there is no such thing as a single choice. A poet especially invents and reinvents a father to fit in with the growth of the poet's mind. Perhaps this claim shouldn't be made for poets alone. Every human soul has to reinvent itself in order to carry on.

When I walked through the snow in 1978 and 1979 it was my father's story-telling voice that I heard most often. A tone of reminiscence that made the whole household stand still, to listen and enjoy: stories of felling trees, of poaching in the Blackwater, of Brunnock's beef, the Cornerstone at Cappoquin, Tom Poole the travelling salesman and Johnny Dubliner who walked the roads between Dungarvan and Lismore every summer, or Paddy Dineen, the process-server, who always managed to climb over estate walls and serve summonses on unsuspecting Anglo-Irish debtors. Many Irish fathers tell stories as a form of inoculation, or balsam, against their darker, unhappy moments. I would dishonour him if I failed to mention that gift of giving stories. I don't think I've inherited that gift. But my sister, Mary, has: she loves the long tale of a personal connection, the tale of some heroic deed among a cousin or a labouring friend of my father's.

The urge to write doesn't always come from the gift of storytelling. It can just as easily come from the effort of *not* telling. The making of poems in my own case comes from my mother's and my grandmother's constant warning to edit the daily happenings in my life. It is a strange poetry, I know, that fears constantly for the health of the reader. In many ways my father was my first reader. Except that I was the father and he was the child. What happened in my childhood was not a matter of indifference to him, but most of my own stories were told only to my mother. Snow is the perfect metaphor for this. One holds certain pains inside oneself in a winterish way, and the pain becomes a thing of stature and strength like a canopy of frozen trees in a photograph:

> *We survive self-knowledge like the memory*
> *of war, or a car crash. Not only ourselves*
> *are victims but those who teach us love.*

('November')

Five Summer Afternoons

In 1986, Máire, Liam Miller's daughter, wrote to say that there were fewer than a hundred copies of my first collection, *The First Convention*, left in print. She planned a new edition – I was going to add ten unpublished poems from 1976 and 1977 to the book. The dying Liam Miller read an earlier version of this essay and approved its inclusion, but as an appendix rather than a preface. Liam had a bibliophile's love of appendices. The death of Liam Miller put an end to the project. Indeed, it was the end of The Dolmen Press. My second book, *The Sorrow Garden*, from Anvil Press Poetry in London was also out of print, by this time. I decided to let the two of them go, "to let the hare sit" as one of our politicians said years ago in a different context.

These poems of mine that won the Patrick Kavanagh Award in 1977 and that were published by Dolmen in 1978 were written mainly in 1975 and 1976, the year of my graduation from University College Cork and the wasted year of the Higher Diploma in Education. For some unknown reason, the Kavanagh Award of 1977 created a stir. There was an amazing, amount of press coverage. It was the *Sunday Independent* that published the names of the panel of judges – a thing that was never done before and I think has never happened since. Whatever the reason I still meet people who know me only as the winner of a Kavanagh Award, despite the fact that I have published four books of poems. The earliest poem in *The First Convention* is 'Her Blindness', first published in *The Irish Times* in 1975.

When I think of the atmosphere of my life at that time, I think of the extraordinary good weather in West Waterford and Cork City; long summer evenings when Cork was filled with that characteristic golden light diffused by the red brick of its buildings; and equally warm summer days when the garden at Glenshelane House, where I had my own writing room, was full of the heavy fragrance of newly planted trees, hydrangeas rescued from undergrowth and blossoming cordylines. As well as the scent of flowers, I recall the smell of paperback novels by Patrick White and Andre Gide – that distinctive smell of paper left too long in the sun.

White and Gide are a rich, mandarin mixture. I'm not surprised that it's taken me so long to unravel my own narrative. The mid-1970s in Ireland were also the years of the first Coalition government of my memory, the years of the murdered British ambassador, the humiliated and later vindicated President Ó Dálaigh and the Bloomsday Election of 1977 that swept Fianna Fáil back to power with an almost unbelievable majority.

A university education provides a youth with my background – rural quasi-working class – with insulation; one is insulated from the forces that swept through one's childhood, political and social. University is the first ivory tower that is given to us: we either use the ivory tower well, like Yeats, or badly like the witch in *Rapunzel*. Campus life removes us from our original context; we are rescued from the swineherds. But in 1975 or 1976 I was completely absorbed into the world created by books – I wandered from campus café to pub to campus café carrying Jeffares's *Commentary on the Variorum Edition of the Poems of William Butler Yeats*. It was my bible. I still think of it as one of the most beautiful books ever created by a scholar. I did none of my assignments, but assembled my own catalogues and bibliographies of favourite writers: A.E., Yeats, James Stephens, André Gide, Camus.

At weekends I returned to West Waterford, not to my parents' house with its practical simplicity, but to Glenshelane House, the Irish home of Denis FitzGerald, a grandson of the Duke of Leinster and direct descendant of the patriot, Lord Edward FitzGerald. When I began to write in my teens, he became the father-figure of all my literary activity. I met him through my brother Michael, who was a radio-electronics student at the time and working weekends in the Glenshelane garden. Denis, or 'The Brigadier' as everyone called him, was a director of the City brokers, Panmure Gordon, and spent most of his time in London. With an arrogance germane to young Irish poets, I persuaded him to take all my adolescent scribblings to the London office to be typed and photocopied by his secretary. On my twenty-first birthday, he bought me my first typewriter. For twenty years he has remained my constant sparring partner in politics and poetry. From London, too, in the early and mid-1970s he brought back to West Waterford the excitement of several English political crises – the demise of the Labour government, the negotiations over Zimbabwe, the sterling crisis and the Heath-Thatcher rivalry. His companionship, therefore, lifted me out of the context within which I grew up; the world he offered was also an education, an ivory tower.

When I think of the atmosphere of my life during the writing of *The First Convention,* therefore, I think of conspicuous interludes on hot days, four or five summer afternoons in Cork City or Glenshelane. I think of the day Theo Dorgan and I arranged a daft poetry reading in the Old Presbyterian Church with free flower seeds for everyone, or the days we spent looking at Michael Ayrton's Minotaur sculptures in Lavitt's Quay, which resulted in my 'Daedalus, the Maker' and a series of Minotaur poems from Theo. Theo published his own small booklet *A Slow Air* a month before I published my own pamphlet, *Shattered Frost,* in 1975. I was more methodical than he, having gotten the names of one hundred people who promised to buy the chapbook. I doubt if I could do better than that today.

Meanwhile, back at Denis FitzGerald's house, I met people like Muriel Spark and Molly Keane. Miss Spark was travelling through Waterford and Tipperary with the handsome Brian de Breffny, later Baron de Breffny. They had been part of the expatriate Anglophone community in Rome that had included such Irish luminaries as Desmond O'Grady, Denis Devlin, and Seán Ó Criadáin. Muriel Spark hoped to find a house in Ireland. Molly Keane, on the other hand, hadn't yet achieved the public triumph of *Good Behaviour*. She lived in a kind of twilight zone of reading and gardening, and caring for the pig-like chihuahuas that always accompanied her in her old Morris Minor. I remember those days vividly, but not as if they belonged just to memory. They are more like remembered paragraphs from a favorite novel. I can easily recall the absolute dead heat of the garden in Dervla Murphy's house at 'Clairveux' in Lismore on the day we first met. Rachel, her little daughter, was naked in the heat. Dervla herself had stripped to underwear, and her body radiated what I perceived at the time as physical and moral health. I was right. If I am too attached to the atmosphere of the first book, it is only because it brought me a great deal of good luck – luck that lasted a whole year, from the Patrick Kavanagh Award in 1977 to the Iowa International Writing Fellowship in August, 1978,

When I came up to University College, Cork, in the autumn of 1972 I was not impressed by the place. I loved the library, the atmosphere of the Aula Maxima, the fine shrubs in the president's garden, but intellectual companions were slow to materialize. I had read four books of modern poetry at that time, Murphy's *Sailing to an Island,* Tom Gunn's and Ted Hughes's *Selected,* Ginsberg's *Howl* – a gift from the Chatterton biographer, Linda Kelly – and a PEN anthology. I expected to see other undergraduates carrying these books and devouring them with their coffee and cakes. Instead, the students were just devouring each other, fooling around, larking in the lecture theatres. Being normal. I decided that there were no poets in the place. While in secondary school we had studied the social-realist stories of O'Connor and O'Faolain, so I'd already decided that Cork was not a city of poets. The short-story writers must have forced the poets to flee. Lucy's *Five Irish Poets* from Mercier Press was the only foothold that Cork poets had on the literary ladder – that, and the constant appearance of Patrick Galvin's new poems in the English Catholic Journal *The Tablet* and the Belfast magazine *Threshold.* Galvin was not in town, but he had left his surreal imprint and his fateful music. One can find echoes of that music and that surrealism in the work of Gerry Murphy and Robert O'Donoghue. O'Donoghue, who also produced a fine poet in his son, Gregory, ploughed a lonely furrow in Cork. His articles in the *Examiner* and *Evening Echo,* along with his editing of a literary page, was the nearest thing that Cork could get to its own literary magazine. A few miles outside the city lived Seán Ó Riordáin, the greatest Munster poet of all. His gifts were hidden from many because of his use of the Irish language, but the young Gaelic poets, the famous *Innti* group, were well aware of him.

The death and funeral of the composer Seán Ó Riada had a stunning effect on many of the poets who were advancing into middle age. Part of the *Mise Éire* generation, they identified with him completely, so that they were even more deeply drawn into the world of elegy and disappointment. Montague's *A Slow Dance* and Lucy's *Unfinished Sequence* are haunted by the ghost of Ó Riada. It is strange, then, that the death of Ó Riada barely shaded the bright sunshine that was blazing down on the tyro poets.

Youth is cruel, I think, and concern over death seemed too middle-aged to be of artistic interest. Yet, I think we absorbed an atmosphere, and a skill with elegy that more properly belonged to people who were older. After Ó Ríordáin and Ó Riada died there developed a kind of free-masonry of remembrance. It is true, though, that a gap opened between ourselves and our elders (those immediate elders being Montague and Lucy). We wanted leaders who would feed us imaginatively and technically. Like most young poets in the Anglophone world, we turned elsewhere, and mainly to Ulster poetry, to learn technique. It is true that new writers can pick and choose from any tradition. We did pick and choose. From Ulster we picked conservative techniques in writing, but from the Penguin Modern Translations we chose wider political convictions.

We used to gather regularly in The Long Valley, Humphrey Moynihan's lovely bar near the General Post Office; we gathered to hear the latest tales from the Ulster Movement. John Montague would usually have some piece of first-rate gossip about Heaney or Mahon or Longley. Pat Crotty would regale the company with stories of Scottish writers – he was doing postgraduate work on MacDiarmid. Theo Dorgan would sit down briefly, agitated like a Cherokee scout, with two or three projects in his head. He had the self-absorbed confidence of all the natives of Cork City, a confidence that pervades the poets from Galvin to Lucy to the young Patrick Cotter. The star of Heaney was rising at this time, of course, and with it the destiny of all Ulster poets. It was like the rising tide of Lemass's economic programs, something astonishing and beautiful to behold – rendered even more beautiful, I think, because we could never be part of it. Montague kept us informed about his fellow Ulstermen with a mischievous good humor. Some of the young poets were depressed about this Ulster ascendancy, which just goes to show how ignorant young poets can be. Anyone who cares to study the documents, so to speak, will see that Ulster was due a break. The Dublin-centered literary scene had almost asphyxiated the reputation of Ulster poets like

Louis MacNeice and John Hewitt. Even if "the Troubles" hadn't broken out in the late 1960s, natural justice would have worked its way to the surface and thrown the spotlight on the older as well as the younger Ulster generations. But the unnecessary panic that a young Munster poet felt was infectious and affecting.

I remember walking out of the exam room after one of my papers in the summer of 1975. I had answered four questions on modern poetry by using Raymond William's book *The Country and the City*, a brilliant work of literary sociology. I felt pleased. The sun was shining. I had done a good paper, good enough, I felt, to earn a tutorship. I saw a poet acquaintance, one of Montague's favorite young poets, coming towards me. He was carrying a new book and seemed excited.

"I'm finished!" I shouted. "The exams, I mean. Is that a new book of poems?"

"It is," he replied. "It's Heaney's new one. He calls it *North*. That's pretty cheeky, isn't it?"

"Christ, give us a look at it."

I took the brand new book from him. On the blue front cover was a drawing of a Norse ship and on the back a full-length portrait of the poet by Edward McGuire. The book would become famous over the next year, selling 16,000 copies and winning the W H Smith Award. The poems were hard and splintered, like shards from the archaeological theme that Heaney had uncovered.

"Is it good?" I asked stupidly, because I could see that it was terrific.

"Unbelievable," he said. "Solid as the big bloody boots in the McGuire portrait."

"Is it as good as *Wintering Out?*"

"At least as good," he said in despair.

"Why are you so depressed?" I asked, "if the book is so good?"

"We'll never be able to write like that. Never. Never."

He spoke like a man who'd been told that he would never walk. He looked over my shoulder. He was disappointed that I didn't share his mood, a mood that I now recognize as a prelude to a really good night's drinking. He saw another poet approaching, someone less naïve. "Must go," he said. I gave him back the book. It was five o'clock in the afternoon. If I ran into the city, I could make a bookshop before it closed.

"Have you written anything yourself?" I asked politely.

"Ah, feck off," he said, and then, as if regretting the harshness of it, he added, "A few of us are meeting in the Valley tonight, if you want to come along."

"Thanks," I said. But I knew I wouldn't go. By the time I would meet them in the Valley they would be drunk. Morose. Defeated, not like young poets who should be studying the masters and learning to walk. "I'll see you there so," I lied.

I can still see him walking away from me. Then I didn't understand what was wrong, but now I do.

The life experience of a young poet is incredibly limited, so limited that would-be poets believe that they must repeat the life experiences of successful writers in order to achieve the authentic state of true poet-ness. We confuse biography with art. The life-and-death situation in Ulster gave Northern poetry a sense of urgency. It was as if poetry were already there, within the political context, disembodied, waiting to be embodied by poets. The defeated young poet who walked away from me that summer afternoon was like the young Stephen Spender in *World Within World* who regretted that there were no great causes left to fight for. We learned that Ulster poets had faced physical danger; we hungered for the personal details behind poems. Like the pilgrims who go to Rome in search of God, we thought that poetry, like God, was located in that particular time and place.

Unfortunately, the uncovering of poetry is a far less romantic task; literature is in the bits and pieces of every day. The pilgrimage that each poet makes is made alone, into personal subject matter. If civil conflict and politics is part of a poet's myth, then so be it; but they are only part of the broad crusade of possible themes that include love, death, loss, rage and disappointment. A wounded young poet in Cork might have found strength in the existentialism of Sean Ó Riordáin; he could have found verbal ferocity in the translations of Frank O'Connor or deep working-class *duende* in the poems of Patrick Galvin.

When we began to publish in the mid-1970s, therefore, Ulster poetry was at its zenith. Montague, Heaney, Mahon, Simmons, Muldoon were names that burned brightly, like fiery crosses in the mist of Irish literature. Wandering around the sun-baked streets of Cork, we couldn't share their energy. We were softened by the kindlier jurisdiction of the Dáil. We did get some stimulation. Both Hugh MacDiarmud and Robert Graves, legendary poets, were enticed to Cork by John Montague. Along with the young poets Seán Dunne, Greg O'Donoghue, and Bill Wall, I had dinner with Graves in *The Oyster*. Graves displayed his box of magic mushrooms and gave everyone the famous Conventry Patmore pat on the head. Hugh MacDiarmid give a sensational reading. It was one of the great literary events of my life so far. The biggest lecture theatre in the university was packed while he spoke with the authority of a Papal Nuncio. At the time, I had read only the *Selected Poems* of Graves, and I hadn't read 'To Circumjack Cencrastus' or 'On a Raised Beach' by MacDiarmid, so I took these poets on Montague's word. The more I read these poets, the more impressed I became by their noble understanding of the poet's role. MacDiarmid's *Lucky Poet* and Graves's *The*

Crowning Privilege should be an essential part of any poet's baggage.

There is a tendency now to play down the role played by Montague in Cork at that time. Certainly poets emerge out of their own energy mass; they cannot be "created" by another individual. But it is impossible to exaggerate the effect of Montague's presence. He had the holy status of an "Ulster poet", the real thing. A nod of approval from him meant a great deal to younger writers. especially to those in his inner circle, Gregory O'Donoghue, Maurice Riordan, and Patrick Crotty. The Waterford natives, Seán Dunne and myself, were in the Junior ranks and the outer circle. But we were pleased to hold that position. New collections of poetry came our way, our attention was drawn to reviews. We were made familiar with the activities that are the norm in a literary life.

The interesting thing about this is that there is a great difference in technique between Montague and most of the other Ulster poets. Montague writes in a difficult reductive process style – a technique that I now like to call "the Dolmen mandarin style". It is a combination of the French Éluard line and the American line-breath of Williams, Pound, and Duncan. It is more formal, less open, than the Black Mountain line, but it is not the iambic, nor does it make use of the ghost of the decasyllable. One can find this Dolmen mandarin style in the poems of Kinsella, Montague, Richard Ryan – who carries it to its highest technical possibility – in Paul Muldoon and such poets of the Dolmen diaspora, as James Liddy and Barry Callaghan. One of the characteristics of the style is the use of the ampersand instead of the full word "and". If one looks at the poems published by tyro-poets in Cork in the mid-1970s one can see the influence of that Dolmen style.

As we read more and more in Ulster poetry, most of us moved away from that Dolmen style. The technique of Longley, Heaney, and Simmons had the familiarity and accessibility of freshly baked bread. When Bill Wall, Seán Dunne, and I started the Poetry Workshop at UCC we were trying to emulate the Hobsbaum workshop in Belfast. The poets who were closer to Montague had an informal workshop going with him all the time. Gregory O'Donoghue, who was my tutor, had his first collection *Kicking* published by Gallery Press, so he was already too "developed" to go into a workshop situation. Our workshop soon began to fall apart because of a lack of some authority figure, so we asked Montague to direct a few sessions. My poems 'Death By Fire' and 'The Recall of FitzWilliam' survived a workshop in his house in Grattan Hill.

Setting up a workshop is one way of dealing with a shared conviction that one lives in a backwater. We developed an elitist workshop attitude to the poem – the conviction that a poem could be constructed so flawlessly that it became unassailable. Poems like 'Daedalus, The Maker' and 'State Funeral' in *The First Convention* grew out of that conviction. The "flawlessness" was not just a matter of excellent meter or regular syllabic count, but the aptness of the phrase. The "necessary phrase" was the fulcrum around which the poem moved. In a workshop, one is always forcing changes in the phrase – that is, in the way the idea is stated or the image built up. Rhythm and structure are the more personal, mystical aspects of the poem's make-up. But the flawless phrase is something that a group, a committee of poets, can share and change.

In those summer days of 1976 and 1977 my head was ablaze with the notion that a poet could make a poem so opaque and iron-clad that a critic who bounced off it would suffer serious injury. I also had an architectural obsession with the "look" of a poem: a poem should be a solid block. This obsession explains the chunkiness of poems like 'Winter Visitor' and 'Greatrakes, The Healer', as well as a number of poems in *The*

Sorrow Garden and *The Non-Aligned Storyteller*. It was only recently that I changed my mind about the way a poem should be finished. Now I think that the making of poems is more human, holistic. A poetry workshop is just that: a workshop. It's not the real maternity unit of poems, no more than the literary pub. Poetry comes from a kind of magic humanism: a great crush of detail presses in upon the poet's life. It is a technical part of the poet's vocation to organize these details, to build the myth of oneself. And myth, as Aristotle noted, is the arrangement of the incidents.

Fifteen years ago I tried to make hard poems because I needed to create something that was harder than myself. I needed to uncover the steel in myself. The fact is, there was never a softer, more romantic undergraduate. I loved wide serpentine conversations that lead nowhere. Theo Dorgan and I used to engage in conversations that were really verbal hallucinations. I recall Seán Lucy's favorite quote about poetry: "Poetry is language at its most intense." Unfortunately, our poems lacked technical intensity, and could never compete with the intense attraction of all-night talking.

It has always been the curse of Cork City that it is incapable of supporting a literary magazine. There is only a limited supply of money. Even David Marcus had to write a novel to pay off the debts of his Cork magazine *Irish Writing*. Without a magazine, literary conversations never get recorded, and young writers never get the chance to develop a professional attitude towards commentary and reviewing. For two decades there has been that lack in Munster. The gossip we know is the gossip of elsewhere. The fruit of our own talk – essays, letters of protest, reviews, parodies and diaries – has never been committed to paper. Lyric poems especially require a written record from elsewhere in order to be fully decoded. Then, they suddenly open, like an oyster, when dropped into the saltwater of a context. The poems in *The First Convention* are only minor glosses made at the edge of more powerful hallucinations.

When I graduated from University College Cork in 1975 1 tried to prolong my stay on campus by doing the much-maligned Higher Diploma in Education and, later, signing on for an MA. I finished the 'Dip" but had no intention of teaching. I published two pamphlets of poems, *Shattered Frost* and *A Warm Circle*. I hoped to get a tutorship in Modern Poetry and refused an offer of postgraduate work in archaeology to keep myself free for tutorials in English. Unfortunately, I never got those tutorial hours. The letter refusing me my tutorship arrived in the same post that confirmed my winning of the Patrick Kavanagh Award. It was the autumn of 1977, a bitter-sweet morning in my life.

Between 1976 and 1978 I studied Daniel Corkery and Theodore Roethke. As my commitment to writing deepened, I veered away from Corkery and his tortuous late works of propaganda. In the end, Corkery believed that the future lay in *Muintír na Tíre* and small local communities. As I had just escaped from a small rural community, that scenario was too depressing. The irony of it all is that Corkery began in a blaze of promise. The early stories and the long novel *The Threshold of Quiet* uncovered a distinctive new world, the world of urban, lower middle-class Catholicism. It was O'Connor and O'Faolain who completed the promise of the early Corkery. What his career lacked was a second novel – and a third and a fourth novel. In other words, a commitment to the imagination. The American Roethke, on the other hand, had too much imagination. His journals and poems were ablaze with demons and angels. While I studied these two writers, ostensibly for an MA, I returned to Glenshelane House where Denis FitzGerald had finally retired. I put to use the one money-making skill I possessed, the skill of gardening. I lived a solitary life, but it was a busy solitude. I earned my keep by working ten hours a week in the garden. I wrote two long postgraduate essays but never submitted them. The reality of an academic life faded into the past. On the strength of a few poems in *Cyphers* and *The Irish Times* I decided to become a full-time writer. I wanted to be a professional like Dervla Murphy: yet, she had warned me that she could fill a barn with all her rejection slips. The truth is, one hardly ever *decided* to be a full-time writer; writers just wake up one morning and find themselves without a more lucrative job.

But I wrote my poems and began to review poetry for *The Irish Times*. First, Terence de Vere White and then Brian Fallon shoved some work in my direction. I survived. Many of the poems were composed while I was mowing. Lengthy bouts of power-mowing created a perfect cocoon for thought. To this day I seek out power-mowers, the smell of petrol, the mixture of gas fumes and mulched grass. Even the vibrating metal shakes the quotidian world from one's shoulders and frees the muscle of writing. By June, 1977, I thought I had accumulated enough poems for a collection. While I was typing the poems up for submission to the Patrick Kavanagh Award people, my father died. His death left me stunned, just how stunned I was too young to know. He wasn't supposed to die, not yet. Only a few days before his death we had been larking around in the garden at home. My father and I were emotionally similar, both soft Pisceans. My father had lived a more successful dream-life, or should I say, *fantasy-life*, than most artists. He was very intelligent but emotionally weak. Since he suffered a major breakdown when I was nine or ten, he had lived like a respectable Victorian antiquarian. He would have been the ideal manager of a mildly successful antique shop. He painted, he studied engineering, he studied astronomy, he obtained some qualification in accountancy – all this time living off a dwindling capital in the bank and a small pension. It was my mother who held the family together, the usual long-suffering, disappointed, forgiving Irish mother. Yet, she had fought hard to get my father. She broke rules. When she first saw my father, he was in uniform, home on leave from Rineanna, now Shannon, and she was engaged to be married to his brother. I didn't learn this until the day of my father's funeral. "The minute I saw him," she said, matter-of-factly, not emotionally, "I knew I wanted him, not your uncle." The first poem in *The First Convention,* 'Stranger, Husband', describes that meeting.

If postgraduate work at university is really protracted adolescence, then the death of a parent is surely the end of that phase of one's life. My father's death was a bitter blow. He constantly annoyed me with his persistent, unreal ambitions. We fought about politics: he was much less conservative than his sons. My mother's grief was also a harrowing thing. She died eighteen months later, of grief. After my father's death, I began to apply for "ordinary" jobs. I abandoned the fantasy of being a full-time writer. Eight months after my father's death, in April, 1978, I started work at Cork City Library. Regular work is a protection against various forms of loneliness. It is also a source of stimulation, something to do with "one's feet firmly on the ground". It also protects a poet from that confusion of destinies, the personal destiny of the poet, the looser destiny of the poems. In the seventeenth century, a correspondent wrote to the Waterford scholar Luke Wadding: 'I have no interest in ye man for he dwelleth in Mounster.'

Celtic Tigers, Mad Cows and Exiles

Despite the weeks of beautiful sunshine in April '97, I think of this as one of the stormiest winters of my twenty-year sojourn in Cork. Winter has served to remind me, yet again, that rain is a weak metaphor for the Irish experience. Rain is too soft. In the last two decades our Irish character has moved from one of soft rain to one of hard weather.

We live in an island now that is well-rigged for heavy weather cruising. When did this change begin? How did our character change so quickly? How can the world have missed our change of character in these two decades of the European Community?

Yes, we have changed. I am old enough to remember an Ireland of the late 1950s. I remember the smells of the houses, especially the labourers' cottages of Twig Bog Lane and Barrack Street in Cappoquin, County Waterford. I was five years old in 1959, throwing sods of wet turf in the half-door of an old woman's house in Twig Bog. Letting my older brother take the blame.

The small town of my childhood had hardly changed since the Great War. In fact, it had really not changed substantially since the Great Famine. Society had stood still. A kind of vapour of indolence hung over the small shops, the kind of vapour, or life as soft rain, that has been captured so well in novels like *The Quiet Man* or *The Country Girls* or even in Cork City novels like *The Threshold of Quiet* or *Bird Alone*. Sociology never quite captures what Ireland was like. To know Ireland you have to use the more precise sciences of fiction and poetry.

But now we have this new label, *The Celtic Tiger*. Who is responsible for this new kind of idiocy? Which Public Relations consultant (briefing which Chamber of Commerce) had the alcohol level to call our tiny, marginal and highly vulnerable economy a *tiger*?

How long will the Celtic Tiger label survive I wonder. At any moment I expect someone on the radio to say that A Sense of the Celtic Tiger Festival has been organised for Prague or Paris or Boston. We are that shameless. We allow people to do these things to us. But let me go to London in 1980, to that Sense of Ireland Festival. After I read poems at the Poetry Society nearly twenty years ago, there was a reception at the Irish Club. I was soon button-holed by a middle-aged man holding a pint of Guinness:

"Yoosir, so you're the Capperken pote," he said, very annoyed.

He had an interesting accent, half-Waterford, half-Kilburn, like many of my relatives. It was the mark of an exile. "Tell may, do de fockine Nuns and de fockine Major still fockine run de town a Capperkin? Do dey?"

It was more than a question. An educated person would call it rhetorical. On that night in 1980 I was only conscious that the man was pure-blind drunk. I never feel comfortable with drunks. This discomfort has been a great impediment in my life. It is not proper for a poet. Nor does it honour the link between drink and exile, and how one may make the other bearable. But I had an uncle who drank too much. Indeed my father drank too much until the day he became teetotal.

In Ireland, generally, there have been two classes of person: those who drink and those who clean up afterwards. I've seen too many busy and exhausted mothers cleaning up. My own mother, for example.

But that night in London I could see the rage in the stranger's question. It registered with me, it was an assignment in sociology. This man was an exile from my hometown, one of the hundreds of thousands who had fled the sinking ship of Éire in the post-War years. The Celtic world he knew was a dead cow rather than a wild tiger. The Cappoquin he fled was a depressed ex-garrison town, poor and congested since the mid-nineteenth century. The "nuns and the Major" was his shorthand for the two dominant presences, The Convent of Mercy and Cappoquin House, home of the Keane Baronets. At that moment in the London Irish Club I could feel two different Irelands.

Here was just one schism in our cultural consciousness. In terms of class origins that exile and I were brothers, absolutely one being. But something had happened in less than half a generation to make us remember our hometown in utterly different ways.

What had happened was the first Celtic surge, the Ireland of the Sixties with its better social welfare system and its free education. I didn't have to leave Cappoquin Station at the age of thirteen, like my cousin John who left for Coventry, England in 1963. I was able to spend five years in St Anne's High School, the local Convent of Mercy Secondary, among nuns who I absolutely adored and who adored me in return. And then University, a rare treat for a country boy.

The drunk who stood over me unsteadily had never had a chance to look twice at his own native land. At twenty-six in 1980, I had already had a first, second, even third look at my hometown and my native country.

For someone born poor in Ireland, even from a warm Fianna Fáil neighbourhood, a University education had the same function as a long prison sentence. University gave me some quality 'time out' to think about myself and my background. UCC in the Seventies was a revisionist paradise.

Many of my friends were following Conor Cruise O'Brien into the Labour Party. I didn't quite 'go over' to the side of the thinking middle-class, but poems I wrote, 'State Funeral' and 'Last Days in the Party' show a sufficient distance from Fianna Fáil values to be almost Seventies Labour lyrics. I see these lyrics now as efforts written to impress the imaginary keeper at the prison gate. There was no prison. There was no keeper.

But the belief that there were forces arrayed against me was a powerful kind of faith. It is the kind of belief that makes forty per cent of Irish people vote for Fianna Fáil (the Party of origins) instead of Labour (the Party of agendas and policies). I am interested in those voices of origins, atavistic, personal, overwhelming. For that reason I listened to my Cappoquin exile, his rage and his loaded breath. He wasn't interested in my poem about Michael MacLiammoir at Cappoquin or the fact that Cappoquin was named by James Joyce as the hometown of Molly Bloom's would-be Gibraltar lover in *Ulysses*.

What my Irish exile wanted was to hear a litany of the names he hated, so that he could expectorate his sense of betrayal and grind it into the floor of the Irish Club. I failed him. But I cannot forget him.

The pain of exile must be worse than the frustration of living in the Irish Republic. The success of the Irish economy today is due to the voluntary self-exile of surplus labourers over a long period; and not just labourers, but doctors, technicians, even educated children from (God forbid) respectable families. They have gone so that the rest of us whose snouts were already in the feeding-trough could get fat in peace.

So, when I hear the expression Celtic Tiger I don't reach for my revolver, I reach for my handkerchief. I weep for the arrival of yet another neat cliché of Irishness that will prevent outsiders from knowing us. Ireland, like America or Canada, is a tentative compromise of interests. The welfare state that educated me is slowly being withdrawn from working-class terraces. The tax code is simplified so that the rich can keep more of their money while welfare legislation becomes more difficult to understand. It is not yet a sin to have no job, but we are getting there. Privatisation is on the agenda. The social good of mighty companies like Bus Eireann and Bord na Mona has been removed from the Balance Sheet.

In a marvellous twist of fate, the Dáil has ceded authority for its citizens' well-being to the European Commission, having only recently wrenched such authority from the British and the Hierarchy. Perhaps we never wanted national independence in the first place. Perhaps that is the nub of our nature, and it has driven our national and international policy for two decades.

And then, today, a surprise phone-call. My brother, Michael, wants me to come back to my native town for a meeting to discuss the editing and publication of a book to mark the millenium in Cappoquin. A book, therefore, to haul together all the strands of Cappoquin memory.

Is such a book possible? I mean, is it possible to publish a non-fiction book that would say everything about the past of an Irish parish?

My brother tells me that the meeting will be attended by all those who write things down: the parish priest, a highly educated man, and the school-teachers, those scriveners of every Irish townland, as well as Cappoquin's most famous son, Dr Michael Olden, now parish priest of Clonmel, but formerly President of Maynooth College. Absent will be that drunk man of the London Irish Club, that Senator of the Exiled who left nothing behind him in Cappoquin but a society that oppressed him and an economy without promise.

Who will represent the exile? Should I represent him? Should we light a candle in the window of the commmittee room, like President Robinson who was the first powerful person (since Bishop Lucey of Cork) to give a damn about the jettisoned poor of the country? Or should the memory of the *spailpín fánach*, the wandering Irish labourer – like the memory of the Mill workers of New Hampshire or the Norwegian fishermen of Minnesota's North Shore – should such memory be allowed to run it course and die of irrelevance?

So, we return to the vital questions of remembrance and the Celtic Tiger. Has too much memory weakened us? Should we put the umbrella of an electronics factory between us and our uncomfortable past? Isn't this what we have hoped for and planned for with astonishing confidence?

There is definitely a feeling abroad that the past has weakened Ireland. Or that our War of Independence was somehow a misreading of the past that led to the erroneous creation of a new State. Our position is like that of the post-Gorbachov Russians. Our past is an embarrassment. What we must do is extend our present into the past so that everything is altered to fit in. Everything must dovetail into the needs of our present. We must intern all romantic nationalism, all Irish-centred radicalism, into a cage of Ethnic Studies or Irish Studies. Revolutionary Irishness, inspired by Tone, Connolly, Pearse, is outside the pale of civilised discourse, rather like the IRA characters in a Tom Clancy novel. The question has never been asked: to whose advantage have we revised our history? Who has it weakened, who has it made strong? It is true that since 1969 we have lived in a continuous present; a present that began with the new Ulster Troubles and the Arms Trial and continues with political violence and revisionist history teaching. There is a strong socialisation process involved in the teaching of history. This has never been properly interrogated, either by sociologists or historians.

The past of Ireland belongs to its educated middle-class. I sometimes think that the orientation caused by our War of

Independence was so rural and Catholic that it actually ran counter to our interests, our material interests. For a Southern Irish person nothing of vital interest is ever at stake when history is discussed; certainly no interest with the vitality of an East Belfast Unionist. The Southern Irish only get angry about history when it alienates an English friend or customer. Then you can see the sparks fly. Ironically, all Paudeen's fingers in the greasy till are revisionist fingers. In many ways the kind of vision propagated by old Fianna Fáilers, a free, Gaelic, self-sufficient Ireland, was always only that – a vision. When tested by power, by elected office and Cabinet responsibility, it was found to be unworkable. Not only do we live in an interdependent world, but we live in an interdependent Ireland. Unionists, who live in mortal fear of our dreams, really do exist and really do object strongly. Not to know this is to be perpetually without power in the real sense.

So there.

Yes, there has been a change in memory. The software of our past has been re-bundled to suit the present task of Irishness. The idea of prosperity has overcome the older idea of nationhood. All the exiles who left our shores contribute now to the propaganda of prosperity, just as the exiles in the old IRB, *Clann na Gael* and AOH focused and deepened our sense of nationhood in the past.

The Celtic Tiger is our great new label. It will stifle social envy and unrest with the same thoroughness as the old idea of nationhood. But it can also get us into trouble. At a recent meeting of European Ministers, for example, the ugly face of envy began to show itself. Danish and Belgian Ministers grumbled that Ireland had breached EU guidelines in attracting inward investment. Somebody was very sore about the establishment of a new facility for Boston Scientific in Galway. In Ireland we consider the European reaction to be slightly daft. After all, a German company, Siemens A.G., decided to site a huge wafer fabrication facility in the north of England just after Britian had rejected European laws on working conditions. Much bitterness was felt about that decision, especially in Cork, where Siemens' executives had looked at the harbour area. Another aspect of this Brussel's envy of Irish success is the relationship between the Belgian electronics industry and the higher cadre of European technical advisors. No doubt, there will have to be an investigation some day of that interesting, distorting relationship.

Another aspect of this rivalry for jobs between European countries that has never been fully discussed is the negative impact that the EC has had on Irish jobs. For example: from my house in Montenotte in Cork I can look across the River Lee at a site where 3,000 men once worked in highly paid employment. All of these jobs were lost as a result of Ireland's opening its borders to European trade. I don't have the time to research the names of all the closed factories of the South; to list all the footwear factories, bakeries, flour mills, tyre manufacturing facilities, et cetera that have closed as a direct result of Ireland's open economy since we joined the European Community. The fact that we might have raised a little Tiger from the ruins of these factories through our own efforts has been lost on many of our European partners. I wish some economist would quantify all the jobs lost by Ireland because of European integration.

Most of the men (mainly men) who lost jobs in the Seventies and Eighties in Ireland never worked again. Working in the local Library for nearly twenty years means I've been with these people since the day they lost their jobs. I remember one man's wasted middle age after Dunlops closed. Today he is an old-age pensioner. He laughed when I recently mentioned our Celtic Tiger. "Another shaggin' smoke-screen," he joked. He lives in a Corporation housing estate on Cork's Northside. He has four children, two boys, two girls. His eldest child, a son, landed a job as a Clerical Officer in the Dublin Civil Service ten years ago. That was an amazing stroke of luck, one of those miracles of Maupassant proportions that sometimes fall upon a working-class family.

Things must have looked hopeful ten years ago. His youngest child is now twenty three, but she has never had a job. She is well educated, with Diplomas in Word Processing, Office Procedure, et cetera. The other son and daughter are on the dole. So that family, whose bread-winner became redundant in 1977, has a second-generation unemployment rate of seventy-five per cent. What is unusual about that man's family is that one member has actually got a permanent job.

This is why the Celtic Tiger label is such a dishonest one. Ireland is much more fluid, tantalising, varied, hopeful and despairing, uplifting and depressing – all at the same time. Like any other country, we have myths that buttress our national character and even determine our responses to social and political events.

We are probably unique in that the greater part of our serious intellectual life takes place outside the jurisdiction of the State. Influential outsiders speak about us, tell us how we should live, even correct us when we tell them how we live. Imagine if all the English and American journals were published in Ireland, if all the influential publishers, like Faber, Oxford and Knopf were based in Dublin or Cork? Seventy per cent of everything we manufacture has to be sold outside Ireland. I should think that the same proportion of Irish thought is edited and consumed abroad as well.

What does this mean for our daily life in Ireland? What does it mean for a writer like myself who lives here year-round? Every idea I have about my country isn't conceived for a seminar – it is, rather, a product of one way of life here, a justification for living. To live in one's own place is a constant struggle, between the local and the international, between the anecdotal and the scholarly. A native land is more than a seminar or a clever descriptive phrase. All I can say for certain is that the same present continues, from the Arms Trial of 1970 to the McCracken Tribunal of 1997.

Who knows what tomorrow's *Examiner* or *Irish Times* headline will be. A new factory to feed the Celtic Tiger, perhaps – or a dead mad cow somewhere in a constituency that voted 'No' to contraception.

Whatever animal, Tiger or Cow, that burns through the night, building up the trader in shares and options and pulling down the labourer in its fearful symmetry, it moves out of a dense woodland of memory and remembrance.

I cannot get the London exile out of my head. The Kilburn accent is now such a rare part of daily life in Ireland, such a rare thing, like a corncrake. And when you think about it, getting drunk after a hard day's physical work can't be such a terrible sin. Yet, where do the Irish poor go now, into which pubs may they not apply? The working poor of my hometown are no different from the educated. They breathe the same Cappoquin air and come out of the same bookish Deise earth.

For the earth is bookish around Cappoquin. In the matter of remembrance, my native place has lost out badly in recent years. The town of Lismore, that elegant and educated older sister of West Waterford, has turned most eyes in recent years. Lismore has had its vocal admirers, and its keepers of memory, in Dervla Murphy and George O'Brien. O'Brien's exquisite memoir *The Village of Longing* and Dervla Murphy's *Wheels Within Wheels,* have placed Lismore on the higher slopes of Parnassus.

My native place, Cappoquin, seems to have lost out imaginatively in recent times. The powers-that-be in literature have passed it by. In the Nineties the town itself seems quieter.

Perhaps this is a false impression. After all, Cappoquin people have always been energetic.

The railway station is now closed, the cinema closed, the factory closed, Sargent's Garage: Sargents, Moores, Mansfields, Russells, McCarthys, Ahernes, Kennys, Fennells. Business names disappear. Even places where people were visibly poor disappear, the row of Nuns' cottages in Barrack Street, Twig Bog Lane with its dry toilets and bramble-covered well. Forty years ago babies were born as their parents dreamed of a decent life in these places. I am glad to see them go and I'm glad to see the better public housing in Shanbally; although alarmed at the huge concentration of housing that has been built there.

I think again of that drunk labourer in the Irish Club in London. Maybe I passed him on the street when I was a child. Perhaps he bought five Woodbines in McGrath's shop or had his first pint in Jimmy Foley's Railway Bar. Perhaps he made a girl from Tallow pregnant and fled to England. When I was a child, young men from Cappoquin were always making Tallow girls pregnant. Which is strange when one thinks that Lismore lies between them. Or maybe it isn't. Lismore was always a discreet town. And in the Sixties especially, Cappoquin men were famous for their energy. It must have had something to do with eating all that cut-price, not-for-export bacon from the Factory.

An education is a strange thing. It is like exile, or – as I've mentioned before – like a long prison sentence. In my childhood before the days of the Celtic Tiger my native town was a place of energy, despite the social stagnation and the pathetic inertia caused by the obsession with respectability. The energy was visible. It was a Tigerish thing, youths coming from work in white overalls, Jimmy Brady's maiden-eight rowing crew on the river, practising for a challenge against Athlunkerd or the Garda Club, or a full and busy GAA field on a summer's evening.

But there was another energy in Cappoquin, an energy clearly visible to me as a sixteen- and seventeen-year-old. Even then I knew that my hometown was a town of poets. Padraig Denn, for example, the nineteenth-century allegorical-religious poet. He'd worked as the sacristan in the new Cappoquin Church and translated the Bible into Irish. But his greatest claim to fame was his edition of O'Sullivan's *Pious Miscellany*, republished by Dillon of Cork in 1841. Denn was a scholar, but with a very high moral grammar. Denn was only the first of a whole singing-school of Cappoquin poets. Their names survive for me like individual gardens of remembrance. There was Michael Cavanagh, born in 1827 in Cappoquin. A cooper by trade he moved to America in 1849 and wrote for the *Celtic Monthly Magazine* and the *Boston Pilot*. Like Denn, he knew Irish and wrote translations as well as original poems. Another poet of Cappoquin was John Walsh, once called 'the leading poet of the South of Ireland. He was born at Belleville Park, a place later associated with Molly Keane, in April 1835. He was one of *The Nation* poets, writing under 'J.W.', 'J.J.W.' and 'Boz'.

These were only some of the Cappoquin writers whose names I knew. I revelled in them, at the age of sixteen and seventeen. The books, I imagined, fell like fruit, fell and seeded other books, in the endless process that seemed like remembrance in a garden.

That drunk man in the Irish Club in London in 1980, I discovered later who he was. In Ireland even the poor don't remain anonymous for too long. Which is why it is so difficult to be poor. One has to get away, to improve one's life or to make one's misery anonymous.

We both came from ordinary provincial families. But our notion of this one place, the town of Cappoquin, was so different. His notion was learned from an anthology of humiliations. I knew humiliations too. Being last in line, or almost last. Being passed over. Having to work incredibly hard just to stand still when other children had parents always on hand to prop them upright. Early on I was lucky enough to develop a self-righting mechanism.

But in his life there was no other series of incidents, nothing to teach forgetfulness which is a kind of survival gift. This is the gift in reading. As a child I grabbed hold of a book and ran, as a horse bites into a bit. We have moved on from the Whittaker baby-boom of the Sixties to the two-sibling cubs of the Celtic Tiger. In each individual Irish life there is a story to be told. The accumulated stories do cohere sometimes to create a single organic thing, a biography of the Dáil.

I honour the memory of that lonely man. My sister Mary and many of my cousins know the pain of emigration. Exile is too fancy a word for it. It is emigration. Donal Foley, the Waterford writer, wrote well about the experience fifty years before the Tiger roared:

> 'Bhí na fir go leir ag dul ag togáil sa Bhreatain mar go raibh an saghas sin oibre an uair sin flúirseach. Bhí job agam ar an mbóthar iarann i Londain. Bhíomar ar fad ag teitheadh on dí fhostaiocht. Bhí ar ndothain againn den saol Eireannach.'

When I read this in *Scriobh 3* I wanted to make a poem of it. Such a real experience, such desperation – and bravery caused by desperation:

> *A pound-note was the best kind of passport*
> *In those days, so I held my pound tightly*
> *After my mother turned away. Idlers*
> *Waved farewell from Ferrybank corners.*
> *There was nothing heroic about my*

Thomas McCarthy

Going, nothing like a political destiny.
I'd just wasted a summer standing round
Until a job came up on the Underground.

('The Emigration Trains')

A Poet in the Library

"Oh, go on then. You can take out some adult books."

The words are Mrs Bolger's, the indulgent and wonderful Branch Librarian of the Carnegie Library in Cappoquin, Co Waterford. It is a winter's afternoon in the late Sixties. The noise of the pneumatic hoisters in Sargent's Garage, and the voice of young Michael Sargent shouting to Dick Fraher or Andy O'Keeffe, comes through the Library windows and even the walls. But the noise doesn't disturb either Mrs Bolger or me. The fire is lighting in the Lending Section and I have in my hand the first full poetry collection I will ever read: Richard Murphy's beautiful *Sailing to an Island,* a hardback from Faber & Faber. Mrs Bolger has just broken a regulation: I can borrow an adult book on a child's ticket. "Here, you may as well try this one too. It just came in from Lismore." She hands me a second book, a joint *Selected Poems* from Thom Gunn and Ted Hughes.

In the small Branch Library in Cappoquin Mrs Bolger and I engaged in a loose kind of poetry workshop. She saw the pattern of my borrowing. In a time before the complete professionalisation of the service, she was that most perfect being in the book trade or the arts: a gifted amateur in the service of the public. I think of poetry always as a private matter, a question of material appropriated emotionally and then thought about. Libraries, on the other hand, are public spaces, places of leisure, education, information and *welcome*. There is no earthly reason, none whatsoever, why a user should ever feel unwelcome in the open, democratic, non-judgemental space that is a Library Lending Section. I'll never forget how welcome I felt in that public space in Cappoquin.

For years, therefore, I was a user, a borrower, before I came to work in a library. Cork City Libraries where I now work is a vitally different place from that Branch in Cappoquin. Cork is a great thriving city; its Public Library has over twenty thousand registered members, and probably treble that number of Reference users. Graduate professionals run every department, Archives, Lending, Reference, Music and all outlying branches. There are days when it can be insanely busy, with books and CDs piled high, photocopiers whirring, reference staff running everywhere to satisfy professional, business and leisure users. Exhibitions will be hung, classes in Literacy or Literature given in the Davis Room, parcels of books returned from others Libraries on Inter-Library Loan, reserved books checked and shelved. But always, the physical need to carry books. People with no experience of the book-trade never realise just how physical the whole activity is. A busy library can be both physically and mentally exhausting.

But however busy a library becomes, the principles behind the activity remain the same; to provide a space open to all citizens where they can learn, become informed, browse and feel brilliant – and be entertained with the accumulated work of their own writers and artists. It could be said that the Tax Office is where the State takes something from its citizens, whereas the Public Library is where the State places something back into the community. It is the people present, librarians and users, who constitute the only valid definition of a public library.

It's important to remember that the impulse to make a public library service arose from a sense of duty to society and a firm belief in its consistent improvement. We have a lot to learn from the Victorians. They had fewer delusions than ourselves and they had a wonderful belief in the general power of education. They didn't worry too much about the word 'inclusiveness', but they worked consistently through committees and public appeals to bring something extra into social life. It is salutary to look at the *First Annual Report* of the Cork Free Public Library Service, published in April of 1894:

> Your Committee, therefore, after several meetings, arrived at the conclusion that it was useless to consider the question of a Library until the financial difficulty for providing for its maintenance was overcome. Their attention, however, was called by Mr WJ Lane, M.P., to the provisions of an Act passed a few years ago, called "The Technical Instruction Act, 1889", which empowers municipalities to levy a rate of 1d in the £ for the purposes, termed in the Act "technical instruction" and "manual instruction".

A Committee of notables – The Mayor, High Sheriff, Mr Crosbie, Mr Hill, Mr McMullen, Mr Beamish, Mr FWAllman, Mr Green, Mr Jolley, Mr Knight and Mr Baker – submitted a report which was adopted by the General Committee on June 23, 1892; Aldermen Madden, Roche, Sheehan and Councillor Barry were selected as Management Committee members by the Corporation and a Librarian was elected on September 15, only to resign twelve days later. The first Public Librarian to take up the reins in Cork was Mr Wilkinson who came from Leeds Free Public Library. Two Assistants to the Librarian were appointed in March of 1893 and a Catalogue of Books was printed on May 30th, only three months after the first delivery of books.

In the first year of the Library, Darwin's *Origin of Species* was borrowed twelve times, twice by a dressmaker, once by a stonecutter; Carlyle's *French Revolution* was borrowed on average twice a month, twice by a saddler, three times by a carpenter and three times by a railway engine-man;

Drummond's *Natural Law in the Spiritual World* was borrowed seven times, twice by chemist's assistants, once by a tailor and once by a warehouseman. But the popular authors were as ever the novelists: Dickens', Lever's and Scott's works were borrowed on average over four hundred times. Even in 1894 the Library Committee's worries sounded familiar: 'the Committee's greatest difficulty is their inability to provide books in sufficient numbers to meet the demands of borrowers.'

It all sounds familiar to those who've had libraries at heart for years. What is interesting is that local government officials and luminaries in local corporations were already at work in library provision more than twenty years before the Carnegie Free Library became a familiar landmark in Irish life. Library provision, thank God, has always been seen as a natural consequence of the extended franchise: it is a symbol of proper local government, and public officials who don't provide it are treated harshly by the local electorate.

Working in this most creative branch of local government, I've become aware that a poet is no different from any other librarian or library assistant. I have worked for nearly twenty years in the Public Library service, spending hours on end with colleagues who are as gifted and complex as any novelist or poet. Nowadays, on any staff of, say, ten librarians, you would be likely to find two or three people actively interested in writing, two trained in counselling, two interested in aromatherapy, three or four interested in classical music, two able to play a musical instrument, one or two related to someone already in the booktrade, four or five fluent in a continental language. Most librarians in Ireland are brought up in conventional bourgeois Catholic families where the hiding of talent, especially by females, has been developed into a fine art. Modesty in ambition is encouraged at home, and accentuated by the death-in-life grading system of the Irish Public Service.

In my own case, for instance, I have moved up one Grade in twenty years.

The stability of this culture means that it would take a nervous breakdown for any Irish librarian to expose the full range of their innate brilliance and education. Lukewarm tea, as Daniel Corkery pointed out in *Threshold of Quiet*, is what it's all about. Cocky or pushy people are generally shunned. The demands of the reading public accentuate the stable modesty of librarians. The borrower, as anyone who has dealt with this vital creature must know, demands consistent service, rapid turn-around in the queue and no nasty surprises. It would be difficult to give library users a regular service if all librarians started acting like inspired geniuses, disappearing all at once to finish the vital poem or make notes for the novel. Ironically, librarians and the reading public understand each other perfectly. Borrowers prefer to find genius in books; a genius behind the lending desk would only interfere with the borrower's relationship with the books on offer.

But a public library should always be considered a proper preoccupation of any land at peace. In the ancient world, Ptolemy I took advantage of the long peace between Macedonia, Syria and Egypt to set up museums and libraries. It was Demetrius of Phalerum, expelled from Athens, who reminded Ptolomy of the advantages that accrue to a country that builds libraries and attracts men and women of culture. When the chronicler Strabo visited Alexandria in 24 B.C. he found buildings with covered walks, arcades furnished with recesses and seats, dining-halls for scholars in that 'temple of the Muses'. Of the two great libraries of Alexandria, in Brucheion and Rhakotis, the Byzantine scholar Tzetzes estimated they contained over five hundred thousand volumes. The classification of these volumes, parchment and papyrus-rolls, was a literary task. The Head Librarians of Alexandria included Apollonius the poet, Aristophanes the Homeric scholar and

Eratosthenes the polymath. The care of great collections, like the work of history, is something that requires spiritual depth as well as administrative skill. Even in our own time, writers like Archibald MacLeish, Frank O'Connor and Philip Larkin have carried on that tradition of learning coupled with public duty. It is my hope for the future that public libraries will attract the literary and the artistic administrator as well as the computer nerd and the technocrat. Nowadays, it helps to have a Doctorate in Information Science, but librarianship without the personally developed feel for books, their past and their spiritual cost, is a truly sterile task.

My own love of books comes from my father. My abiding image of him will always be of a slightly stooped, prematurely greying man at ease by the window with a book in hand: *Carter's Advanced Accounts* perhaps, or a Zane Grey Western. Men who read Westerns are a dying breed. I regret their passing, their steady, long-suffering silence, their spiritual, westwardly soul-searches where a man could befriend a lively colt and converse with tumbleweed. In literature, there is now no place where the moderately educated man can go to repair his soul. It is Tom Wolfe, Terry Pratchett or nothing. There are now no books that are the literary equivalent of a large bottle of stout. Men have lost out in the area of popular fiction because they never took care to buy enough books.

I first went to work in a library when I was an undergraduate at UCC in the mid-Seventies. I had a weekend job as Honorary Branch Librarian in a disused church in Villierstown, Co. Waterford. Each Saturday I stamped out forty books. The lending section was housed in the choir gallery, from where I could hear the crack and plop of snooker being played in the sacristy. There was something very Larkin-like about that nightmare. Mrs Hayes, the then Waterford County Librarian, supported the project with a kind of bemused enthusiasm because it was part of an early community development scheme. My most famous borrower (as we say in the trade) was Tony Summers, the biographer of JFK and Marilyn Monroe.

I've worked in the Public Library service since 1978, the year my first collection was published. Public librarianship is a leisure service as well as an educational one. When one leaves a University, one steps from the world of *requisition slips* to the world of *request forms*. The difference is crucial: the first has an air of compulsion, the latter contains an anticipation of pleasure. A public librarian doesn't just listen to the conversations that books have with each other, *qua* Borges; he or she has to listen to the conversation of the borrowers.

My own attitude to the reading public is easy-going. The library is an ideal place for a poet to work. A lot of fuss is made about 'accuracy' on the job, but 'attitude' is a far more important gift – I've yet to meet a poet who isn't interested in other people. Poets are insatiably curious and love gossip. But so are the people who read books. In twenty years in the library I've yet to come across a public relations crisis that was caused by inaccurate work. Serious problems when they occur are always caused by poor people management, a surly response and a digging in of heels. For this reason alone the introduction of computers and computer systems into libraries has been a great boon. As computers remove some of the drudgery from searches, they should give us time to be more personal rather than less connected with the reading public. Computers will never do any damage to the traditional library as long as they are used as tools. Many people who market computer systems and software think that the concept of Information Retrieval is something new. In fact, *reading* is one of the oldest, and still the most proven, method of retrieving information. Computers are merely an additional form of reading. The only danger to libraries that is posed by the growth of electronic media is that too much emphasis may be placed upon technology in teaching and recruiting public librarians, to the detriment of training in book conservation, collection building and general humanities. Librarianship like public service is an art, a skill within the humanities, and not a science. I admit to having a prejudice in favour of books. There is no software yet invented that is as good as an enthusiastic, well-read librarian. Books are likely to remain at the core of the Library Service – the condition of the bookstock and its exciting presentation and exploitation is akin to aerobic fitness in general health. From the satisfied reader a whole atmosphere of healthy relationships radiate. As Melvyn Barnes, President of the British Library Association, noted in his address to the 31st Annual Conference in Tralee in 1995:

> There will not be any exciting predictions about the death of the book because millions of people continue to value the Public Library as the key source of printed material. I use the term 'key source' because the Public Library is the only place providing the widest possible choice, without the limitations imposed by the ability to pay.

The astonishing thing about the library service is that it tracks public taste in an up-to-the-minute fashion. Its lending figures when analysed offer the clearest possible picture of public taste. At the moment there are plans and committees afoot to help bring the 'Arts' into the Public Library space. The general readership of the public libraries is not an artistic one, much as I regret to say this. When we discuss bringing the arts inside our spaces we should be aware that for the arts, especially the arts professionals, this will be a new kind of encounter. The newness of it is really the exciting part. The membership of public libraries is much broader, in class terms as well as merely educational terms, than the general membership of Arts Centres. Many of the borrowers of Danielle Steel, Jilly Cooper, John Grisham, Maeve Binchy or Louis L'Amour would be afraid to enter into the Arts Centre next door to our branch Library. The Library is a very familiar space: they feel they own it and that borrowing books doesn't belong to any one particular lifestyle. The Arts Centre (where I happen to be one of the Directors) seems to belong to the trendier young, those who are self-contained and seem to own the future. The hard fact is this – even after you've squandered your future you can still belong completely to your local library. For many borrowers the library is one of the instruments of coping with life, on a weekly or daily basis.

My dream would be that there would be no difference between an arts centre and a library. I imagine something like a pedestrian tunnel between the arts centre and library, and on-line access to the library from the arts centre, as well as a book-centred room, a sort of word factory, within the Arts building for children. There should be more human traffic in galleries and more art in libraries. I am conscious of the richness already in books, but reading a book about art is not the same as coming face to face with a painting. An exhibition has more to do with the artist than the reader. Only when faced with a piece of sculpture or an installation does a reader encounter something radically new.

Nearly twenty years in the library has taught me that poetry is a high priority within a narrow profile of the reading public. One book of poems may be lent in a week when we stamp out 2,000 books of romantic fiction. Poetry is not a popular art, but it has a steady and deep-rooted constituency. I am never angered by the imbalance between the autocracy of numbers and the oligarchy of aesthetic values. Why should I be angry? Each year brings a new poet or two, or a new collection, into the lending section. Poetry may not be as popular as the safer crises of a Mills and Boon, but poetry is constantly renewing itself, even on the shelves of the public library.

One of the privileges of being placed before the public each day is that one can see over time changes in trends and the growth of fashion. At the moment, for example, people have rediscovered Stevie Smith and Pam Ayres. Poets like Paul Durcan, Heaney and Eavan Boland have retained their popularity over two decades. Others, T S Eliot and Frost who were so popular in the Sixties, are now almost completely forgotten by the borrowers in our libraries. Fashion is one of the abiding, tantalising mysteries. Maeve Binchy, Catherine Cookson and Danielle Steel have a ring of permanence about their names. They can look forward to the inexhaustable fidelity of their readers. I know readers who have followed Catherine Cookson from her first book. They marked her early *Mary Ann* pages with ration-books while cutting a slice of bread on the fold-down kitchen dresser; now a zapper for the cable TV rests on the page while they microwave a coffee. A librarian, like a village doctor, shares that enormous intimacy with the public; the knowledge of how life changes for broad groups of the population. One can also see the sociology of one's country worked out in the changing patterns of reading.

The real enemies of poetry are those who think that poems should be as popular as soccer or TV quiz games and as relevant as a political party. Why should it be? We are all terrified of being branded 'elitist' by the new commissars of popularity. It has come to the stage now where I have heard people being praised for *not* having read books. We have to arm ourselves against any morality that forces poets to put on an act of ignorance in order to shine. A poet should stick to the first intuitions, the personal music and the blessed genius of books that protect the integrity of an intellectual life. Working in a library has taught me that creative work is essentially conservative. I don't mean this in the political sense; poets have been among the fiercest radicals, politically and socially. But I use the word 'conservative in its dental, nay, orthodontic, sense: a damning up of life forces, an accumulation of virtues, a hard-packing of memory and rhythm. Most poets are popular on the basis of some fundamental misrepresentation; some sensational piece of gossip or personal tragedy or the survival of political crisis like the Ulster conflict. A poet should not be too troubled by literary public relations. Journalism is most attractive when it is internationalist and progressive, but poetry is most attractive when it is *good* poetry. Poetry is never provincial, only criticism can be provincial. A librarian walking among the bookstacks on a quiet morning sees everything of value conserved in front of him: the great forgotten novels, Scott's *Chinese Love Pavilion*, Greene's *England Made Me*, Sheehan's *Glenanaar;* or the great forgotten poems, Shelley's 'Revolt of Islam' or Cronin's 'R.M.S. Titanic' or Matthew Arnold's perfect 'Dover Beach'. The good librarian takes stock, withdraws, conserves and promotes for the sake of the abundant life within these books.

Ultimately it is a matter of values. Very few librarians are narrow minded; in fact, the story of the public library in Ireland North and South is one of many minor battles against the narrow-minded. The core value is that there should be access to knowledge for all citizens regardless of academic background. The trade union movement and vocational education committees have always been great allies of the public library because both organisations have had an historic commitment to Adult and Continuing Education. Learning is a life-long activity, and the public library will always remain as an essential *vehicle* upon that road. Whether we love poetry or knowledge in general, trades unions will always remain a vital ally and intimate friend of the Library Service. In a 'cut-back situation' (not just a situation, but now an ingrained attitude of local government administration for over a decade) the poor are the first to lose out. The middle-class will always have proportionally more access to academic and professional libraries. Nothing should be allowed to come between the poor and a poem. I was not a child of the middle-class when Mrs Bolger handed me two expensive collections of poetry. She was no socialist, but she had a strong native belief in empowerment.

A librarian's will should be able to withstand the hyperbole of advertising, to fight for shelf space for works of the spirit. A good librarian, like a good poet, should have a mind that stretches over that twilight zone of previous generations. One can never tell when a great book will be restored to its proper context. Television can be a great help. A novel like *Brideshead Revisited* languished in the bland gray wrappers of Chapman and Hall for years until it was released into the public domain through television images. Television will effect the popularity of classics in the future, I've no doubt, so that there will always be an even *popular* reason for libraries to stock the classics. Generally, though, books create their own public. Who could have foreseen the popularity of Noel Browne's *Against the Tide* or Frank McCourt's *Angela's Ashes*? Or Joseph Lee's brilliant history of Ireland between 1912 and 1985? There are certain books that attach themselves to the public heart because of the horror of the contents or the seriousness of the message. I think *Angela's Ashes* is set to become one of the vital Irish documents of the twentieth century. So many Irish people will have read it that a view of society, not just Limerick society, will have been planted in everyone's mind. At one time in our Library there was a waiting list of one hundred and thirty borrowers for McCourt's book. The power of the book is that it offends respectable Irish memory, it challenges silence. In a country that idealises the past with so much soft-focus art and poetry, it offers a fine broad canvas of dry toilets. What's so curious about it is this – most users of the Public Library service are middle-class, who enjoy the book because it releases them from a burden of lies about the Forties and Fifties in Ireland.

As a theme for poetry the library has had very little influence on my own work. The only poem I've written using the library as a metaphor is 'Cataloguing Twelve Fenian Novels'. I got the idea of that poem in the store-room of the Mayfield branch in Cork. We were 'wearing out' old and mutilated stock when I came upon a memo attached to a bundle of Canon Sheehan novels: should they be thrown away or recatalogued? They had come to the end of their useful lives as fiction. The memo was seething with possibilities:

941.591

Rain seeps through the hoarding on the broken window;
Corkery rain, insistent, dramatic.
Youths are playing darts against the library
door, challenging me to respond:
Public servant, hated. Bull's eye!
Tina, these two are gone mouldy, will I
throw them out? A note from Sheila
attached to The Whiteboys *by Mrs. S.C. Hall*
and D.M. Lenihan's The Red Spy –
the red spy a Dublin Castle agent
Forever on the threshold of quiet, of death.

As I spend most of my waking hours in the library, it's only natural that I get ideas for poems while at work. I have to work out a strategy to save these ideas. Contrary to popular belief, modern libraries are bustling places, with a lot of activity and noise. I always carry a few used book-cards (5cm x 2.5cm) in my top pocket. When I returned to the City Library in 1995 after a year in America I was horrified by the total computerisation that had occurred in my absence. The computer meant the death of the card catalogue and the absence of stacks of useful abandoned cards. It's not possible to make notes on the plastic sleeve of a zapper. The genesis of a poem is two or three lines, not necessarily the *first* lines of the poem. But these lines contain the tone and pace of the poem, as well as some crucial irony or insight. At the end of a working week I used to empty out my pocket and sellotape the fragments into a notebook. I like the idea of fragments. We live in a world beyond belief; the only thing we truly share with each other is that lack of belief. Truth, therefore, is a fragmentary thing. Nothing produces a lyric better than a few fragments, moments of cognition and feeling rescued from the brain-dead quotidian world of work. Writing devours time. The grind of a 9-to-5 job and parenthood means that one lives with two fierce editors: work and children. I would not have it any other way. Through those things love weaves its way through our waking hours. Time is hardly ever squandered in my writing because there is little time to squander.

Bad days in a public library can be terrible: constant queues, screaming children, distraught pensioners risking broken bones to beat each other to the latest Maeve Binchy, and perhaps, the boss in foul humour. Suddenly, one can see why Camus abhorred the idea of a regular job, why Yeats loathed the management of men. On such days I envy the poets who went to live on Inisbofin in the Sixties, especially the lucky one who lived with Deborah Tall, or the poets who flee to the sanctuary of the potato-fields of America. Maybe I should give in my notice, take the Boeing to JFK and join Greg Delanty and Eamon Grennan as they wander up and down the Hudson, professing Poetry and distilling the distant elements of home. When a country interferes with intelligent thinking one should say farewell.

Then again, there are exciting days ahead, recitals in the foyer, exhibitions in the Mills and Boon section. In the Public Libraries the best days are only just beginning. Twenty years from now, when every secondary school will have a library and a professional school librarian who will be a key figure in each child's education, when every VEC College of Commerce and VTOS Course will have its fully equipped and brilliantly stocked Lending Section, when there are public library lending sections in Waterstones, Easons and Virgin Megastores, when there are public reading-rooms and reference libraries (instead of vile video games) in each Irish airport and railway station, I will be able to say "I was once a poet in a Library. We endured the great storm of cut-backs in the 1980s, but nobody died."And the young Librarian will nod in approval, because it will be universally understood by then how barbaric, regressive and unthinkable were the cutbacks in the Public Library Service. And this will never happen again, of course. It is unthinkable that the future could ever again threaten the powerful and creative public space that is the library. If the library disappeared, where could the unconnected public go; I mean, those without wealth and connections? The rich and the academically tenured will always have libraries to go to, but the citizen born without privilege depends upon us to keep the portcullis of information hoisted. Those who work in Public Libraries are not so much keepers of collections as scouts who go ahead of armies to find more and quicker routes to victory.

PART TWO

Macalester Notebook 1994

In the Autumn of 1994 I left the busy Lending Desk at Cork City Libraries to take up an International Professorship in the English Department of Macalester College in St Paul, Minnesota. It was a return visit to St Paul for me, as I'd spent several weeks there a few years before as Visiting Writer to the ACTC, the umbrella organisation of Twin Cities Colleges. Many Irish writers already know the city of St Paul as the home town of the College of St Thomas, an institution with strong Irish connections since the heyday of Bishop John Ireland and the nineteenth-century Irish migrations.

More than thirty years ago the then Chair of English at St Thomas, Eoin McKiernan, set up the Irish American Cultural Institute. Over the years McKiernan persuaded wealthy Americans, notably the O'Shaughnessy and Butler families, to endow Lectureships and Literary prizes. The Institute has since moved to the East Coast, but St Thomas has replaced it with a *Centre for Irish Studies*, now the leading centre of Irish Studies in the upper Midwest. Thomas Dillon Redshaw and Jim Rogers now drive that powerful American-Irish engine at St Thomas, organising lecture tours and postgraduate courses as well as editing the *New Hibernia Review*.

The liberal arts college of Macalester is not very far from the University of St Thomas, a fifteen-minute walk perhaps; but Macalester – as its name suggests – has Scottish connections. Indeed, the College itself is an inducted member of the MacAllister clan. 'Mac', as it is affectionately known, still has strong connections with the Presbyterian Synod of Minnesota, the beautifully named Synod of Lakes and Prairies. John Bernstein, a Southern gentleman who taught at Princeton, has been a member of the English Faculty at Macalester for many years. When he and his wife, Cynthia Syme, spent time with us one summer, he suggested that I should take the plunge for one year at least and teach in America. John has taught Irish literature for thirty years. His Department owns what must be one of the very rare prints of a Seamus Heaney film from the early seventies. John has taught Yeats, Heaney, Montague, Edna O'Brien and other twentieth-century Irish writers every year since the mid-Sixties.

When Catherine and I arrived in St Paul we were quite worried; about the children mainly, their health and education. We had a number of scares to begin with – Kate and Neil couldn't begin school until they had all the required inoculations, but we hadn't brought their schedules of immunisation from the Health Board in Ireland; so they had to make two painful visits to the local depressing Rondo Center. They were very brave, taking a battery of jabs with modest protest. It was also difficult to find bread that tasted the same as bread in Ireland. Our son is a real 'bread' man, and he would starve to death rather than eat foreign pastries.

My own idea of St Paul, and of the entire Midwest, came from reading F Scott Fitzgerald. My Minnesota was the landscape of Amory Blaine in *This Side of Paradise* or the streets described by Nick Carraway in *The Great Gatsby*. John Bernstein himself, with his knowledge of good wine and his combative Princeton wit, reminded me of a Fitzgerald character. Also, John had the habit of answering the telephone in the manner of Amory Blaine – 'Lo'.

'Lo, Amory.'

'Lo, Myra.'

Minnesota is the state of Mary Tyler Moore, Jessica Lange, Garrison Keiller and his 'Prairie Home Companion', Robert Bly and Bob Dylan. Now that I've spent a year there, I can recognise the metallic Hibbing accent in Dylan's early albums, and I can appreciate the despairing Scandinavian strength hidden behind the modest gestures and facial expressions of Jessica Lange. Not only those: I can now recognise the brilliant aptness and accuracy of so many Kieller characters in *Lake*

Wobegone. I met some of Kieller's characters every day in the Sundberg Pharmacy, The St Clair Broiler and Widmer's Foodstore in the Mac-Groveland neighbourhood. The literary heritage of Minneapolis-St Paul is especially strong and well-defined.

The Twin Cities is teeming with writers, and not just the Irish at O'Gara's, Cognac MacCarthy's or Kieran's Pub, but Jewish poets, African-Americans, Native-Americans and Asian-Americans. The Irish are always visible to us in Ireland, but it would be an impoverished anthology that excluded any ethnic group. Minnesota in the American world is rather like Cork City in the Irish context – it has committed the mortal sin of being *too far away*. This *too-far-awayness* means that the poets and artists have a strong regional sense as well as the creative duality of those who need to travel a great deal.

I think that the condition of *being far away* has made Minnesotans more intelligent. Minneapolis–St Paul Airport is one of the busiest in America, and Minnesotans are indefatigable fliers. St Paul also boasts one of the best literary bookstores in the world, *The Hungry Mind*, a shop with the character of Kenny's of Galway and the search engines of Blackwells. In many of Scott Fitzgerald's stories and novels there is a strong sense of movement. Home is nearly always perceived as the place of arrival. Fitzgerald describes a feeling, a sense of place, that could be purely Irish. Except that it isn't.

Back in Cork City, just a few years after our stay in America, St Paul and the bright, deadly serious students I taught at Macalester now seem a part of a more perfect *elsewhere*, a mosaic of memories and books. I have before me an album of photographs – my own son and daughter, Neil and Kate, sheltering in an igloo I built for them, both children standing on the ice of Crosby Lake, both in Halloween costume at the 'Zoo Boo' in Como Park Zoo. Many photographs and dozens of books. A place, for me, is defined very quickly by the books it has produced. This, of course, is unfair to the people. Catherine and I made many friends in The Twin Cities, John Bernstein and Cindy Syme, Tom Redshaw (through Tom is an old friend), Jim and Jeanne Rogers, Al Greenberg, Ruth Burks and Diane Glancy.

I have before me now (as I write this down) a photograph of the Macalester playing field, that snow-covered stretch between the Natatorium and the old Humanities, where I walked every morning on the way to teach at Old Main. Catherine must have taken the photograph because the composition is well-balanced; the snow has melted on the footpath that rises away to the left, but still firmly attached to the steep roof of Old Main.

This notebook begins in the week that we arrived in Minnesota. We were shocked by the heat. But by the end of the long Minnesota winter we longed for the heat of high summer again, the buoyant mosquito-laden heat of August by the banks of the Mississippi.

Sunday, 28 August 1994

Our first week in St Paul, Minnesota. A long year stretches ahead of us. We don't know what the months ahead will bring. Everything is different. Even the air we breathe is different. It is probably less polluted than Cork City but has a metallic, oven-dried taste. In time we might find a damp and cool corner that will remind us of Ireland. One thing is certain: we can't go back now. I have a contract to fulfil and our house in Ireland has been rented out for the year. I worry about Kate and Neil. How will they cope? Kate, for example, has hardly spent more than a few weeks without the company of her best friend, Emily Hogan. Now she faces a whole year that will test her bravery. At this moment I feel exiled and utterly disorientated.

If it wasn't for John and Cindy's kindness, we'd be in complete despair. They collected us at the airport and prepared our house, even stocked the fridge. We keep their friendship as close to us as possible, and wear it like a space-suit.

Yesterday Neil and I were playing soccer. We came in exhausted. On the way in I looked at the thermometer. It was at ninety-one degrees. Incredible. And it is nearly September. I think Minnesotans are made of mighty stuff. They are able to survive really hot and humid summers, then woeful winters. I'm not surprised that the people who've taken to this landscape are mainly Scandinavians, people who are used to coping with extremes of climate.

Today everywhere we look there are squirrels, nibbling unconcerned on pavements, in gardens, scurrying away briefly when Neil comes into view. They are beautiful creatures, but at the end of the day they are only rats with fine tails.

We live in an old house on the edge of campus. In the heat of summer its dark and cool corners begin to make sense. Beautiful woodwork, severe and Victorian, like certain old tables in the Convent school of my childhood. In Kate's bedroom, damaged ceiling and really ancient wall-paper, but a beautiful space, with a window looking across the baseball field to the modern Rice science hall.

I love the huge white gas stove in the kitchen, a great enameled winter-defying block of energy. The little tin kettle with a whistle, the pilot lights that go click-click before they ignite. The modest cutlery and china, things understated in a very Minnesotan way. In the basement, two old bicycles, a mighty washing machine that looks like it could have won the Cold War on its own, its face as solid as Eisenhower. And in a dark cubicle, surrounded by a timber lattice-work partition, the hero of every Midwestern home: the central heating boiler. It answers to no one, except the Plant engineers and the High Winds office at the College. We eye it from a safe distance.

America is still the newspaper readers' paradise. Today we got the *Star Tribune*, the *Pioneer-Press* and yesterday's *New York Times* with all its glorious supplements. I was too late to catch the Sunday edition today. The biggest local story is the murder in a parking lot of two policemen. I noticed flags at half-mast everywhere. This is a small community, so the death of two police officers is felt deeply. I can feel the sadness myself and I've only been here a week. Still, we begin to cut coupons from the *Pioneer Press*. Having a jar of coupons is a kind of badge of good citizenship. It's part of the consensus of American life: a vital part of being here.

Looking at Yeats, my paltry notes for September. This is for the course on Poetry and Politics. I've decided to look at Yeats and the Irish War of Independence, Auden and the Spanish Civil War, Robert Lowell (especially 'Notebook') and the Vietnam War, and Heaney and the Ulster Conflict. We will read their key texts, then compare them with the guys who were really involved personally: Pearse, MacDonagh, John Cornford, Charles Donnelly, Berrigan, Bobby Sands and Gerry Adams' fiction from Brandon Books. The huge question that will drive the course (the thesis whose name we dare not mention) is this: Do good poets stay clear of involvement? Or is their involvement a matter of personality, a question of personal loyalty? Are Pearse, Cornford, Donnelly too close to the conflicts they write about to be first-rate poets? It was Pasternak who used the phrase 'radically steep incline' to describe the poet's reading of life, and Seferis, thinking of Stendhal's words, wrote that we live our lives day by day, but daily we don't write our poems. I think there is meat enough for a good course in what I've planned.

Monday, 29 August 1994

Reading the statistics for Minnesota in the *Star-Tribune*. Figures that would make Garret FitzGerald green with envy. Unemployment rate of four per cent, even less in the Twin Cities metro area. A state with a population not much bigger than Ireland, but with two-and-a-half-million people at work. A shortage of labour in many areas, a situation unimaginable in Ireland.

Tuesday, 30 August 1994

A day at the English Department, getting orientated. I have an office that was last occupied by Jack Patnode, a Macalester Professor who died recently. His books still cover all the shelves. They have a beautiful smell, the distinct American smell that comes from different glue and bindings.

A meditative space. The kind of space Seán Dunne would love.

My window is like a window in a monastery, opening onto a tree-lined lawn with the American flag and the Wayerhauser Chapel. The chapel reminds me that this ultra-liberal, ultra-multi-cultural College was once a College of the Presbyterian Synod of Lakes and Prairies. The presiding genius of the place is still Lutheran, an atmosphere that makes me feel comfortable and welcome. Why do I always feel happiest in Protestant atmospheres? Of course, it may be true that only an Irish Catholic, a Greek or an old Communist, could pick up the vibes of a religious culture in accents and responses. The atmosphere connects with something in the past.

At John and Cindy's house in tree-lined Vernon Street. Here also a relaxed, cosmopolitan atmosphere. Intensity of reading, good wine, handsome looks, a flair for life. Yes, I am at home in this blessed corner of Snelling and St Clair. Earlier we walked to SuperAmerica on St Clair, a petrol filling-station, but already our local grocery store. Further up St Clair is Widmer's, a large neighbourhood store famous for its meat. So much comes together in a gas station; it's the equivalent of an Irish pub, but a well-placed Irish pub – across from a railway-station or on a quayside. As Catherine and I sat at a sidewalk table at Napoleon's Café, across the road at SuperAmerica, and watched the comings and goings, the battered Dodges and Mercurys, the sleek Saabs and Volvos, we knew that we'd landed in a different country. We had another *elsewhere* to inhabit and analyse. Intellectually, that's what matters. The sun shone on our corner of St Clair and Fairview. As we drank coffee we watched the sunshine bounce off the concrete bench and its shiny new red and white sign: Edina Realty, Jon Stromme. And from our porch we can see the blinking light of The St Clair Broiler. Across the road, the Sundberg Pharmacy that serves coffee and milk-shakes.

Thursday, 1 September 1994

Today to the Minnehaha Falls, a deep glen cut into a wooded grove between St Paul and Minneapolis. This place reminds me of Killarney, of the Torc waterfall and the romance of Victorian places. Tourism is such a false activity, but the need for it is not false. There is great irony in journeying to places where the imagination has already been. The happiest journeys are the ones that confirm our dream life.

Here in this spot Longfellow reinvented a Native American myth using the form and rhythm of Finnish saga. When I look at these falls I think of Yeats and Sligo – and all the course preparation I've still to do for my classes. Where can one begin with Yeats? Perhaps with the Rose image and all the Pre-Raphaelite English world. In many ways it was Yeats' fine training as an English mind that sensitised his imaginative eye to Celtic things. It was Blake, rather than Davis, who turned him into an Irish Romantic. I can never get T W Rolleston's idea that the English are an Anglo-Celtic, not an Anglo-Saxon, people out of my mind. His arguments for this were very well mustered. In our own day we can see how quickly the English respond to Enya or Edna O'Brien: both women emanate an English kind of Celticness. The Celtic element is as deeply etched into English discourse as Jewish humour is into American daily discourse.

All of these things in my head, spoiling the day. Of course, Longfellow like Yeats was sophisticated enough to mine the lode of gold that was Native American myth.

Saturday, 3 September 1994

To the State Fair. Immense heat, but the constant threat of a thunderstorm. A huge event, thousands of people shepherded through turn-stiles, food-stalls and advertising booths. On the way home the bus conductor was asked about a stop in St Paul. "Heck, I don't know these parts," he said (rather too proudly, I thought). "I'm from Minneapolis. I'm only driving over here during the State Fair."

At the Fair Kate and Neil agreed to be photographed with a boa-constrictor wrapped across their shoulders.

Monday, 5 September 1994 — Labour Day.

Went to Stillwater on the St Croix River with our old friend Tom Redshaw, the editor of *Eire-Ireland* and scholar of all things Irish. An admirer too of Sean Keating's paintings. Like myself, he's intrigued by their Stalinist realism.

Stillwater is an aptly named town, for here the beautiful St Croix opens into a broad pool. Our peace was disturbed only by a lunatic in a small craft called a ski-doo. I watched this man from the shore, worried about him, as if he were a child with a razor-blade.

Stillwater is like Ardmore or Kinsale, but warmer. It just requires a Hedli MacNeice to turn it into a gourmand's paradise. We saw the famous train *The Zypher*, preserved by a local group of railway enthusiasts. Once the centre of the white pine lumber industry, the town is now known simply as the birthplace of Minnesota. The public meeting that founded the Minnesota Territory was held here in 1848. At the Convention, John Catlin, a former secretary of the Wisconsin Territory, became the acting governor of what was then the St Croix Delta.

In times past this area was neutral territory placed between the Ojibway and Dakota peoples. There was endless warfare between these two nations. The Dakota were constantly pushed south and west out of the North Plains by Ojibway who were given guns by French fur traders. In the manner of old Celtic chiefs, like O'Briens or McCarthys, the two Indian nations decided that the warfare would be ended in a single hand-to-hand combat. After a savage battle the Dakota chief killed the Ojibway leader.

We had lunch in The Dock Cafe, extremely good food. And in the men's toilet, a nappy-changing facility. Definitely not Ardmore. I phoned my brother Michael from a public call box, using my MCI call-card for the first time. He was shocked to hear my voice.

Saturday, 10 September 1994

Reading Yeats again, sitting on the steps in front of our house while the construction workers continue their clean up. Something incongruous about Yeats under a clear blue sky. There is so much local reference in Yeats. How can a group of young mainly Scandinavian-American students appreciate all these local references? I suppose to teach well is to localise the experience, so that the student thinks the poem is written with him or her in mind. A poem like 'The Ghost of Roger Casement' or 'Upon a House Shaken by the Land Agitation' is so full of local political feeling that to communicate its full excellence requires several leaps of imagination on the part of American readers. Reading Yeats again I am reminded of the pleasure I got as a student at UCC from Norman Jefferies Commentary on the Variorum Edition. Like FitzGerald's *Omar Kahyam* or *The Decline and Fall of the Roman Empire*, it is a work of art in its own right. Because of the atmosphere of Jefferies I always think of Yeats scholars as a kind of priesthood. Certainly, this is the way Yeats would have it.

Monday, 12 September 1994

Storm

Nothing as electric as a St Paul storm
ever passed my window.
We shiver in our light sheets.

The whiplash of September overhead
is like a conscience catching up:

'What did you do with your Party?
and childhood,
and money, and opportunity,
where have you scattered them?'

Thunder rattles the bedroom windows.
It passes by like a disgruntled Puritan.
When I think our son is crying
it is only the bus on Snelling and St Clair –
its cranky, uncomplicated whine.

Tuesday, 13 September 1994

This evening we watched another electric storm over the college. We were snug in the TV den of our house, but with the blinds up and the house shaking. The sky was a blaze of blue, an electric blue of many sheets of lightning. The lights flickered like candles. Between sheets of lightning, jets were landing every minute or so, coming in low and slowly. Such a dangerous, inspiring sight. We marvelled at all these St Exuperys coming home from the small airports of the Dakotas and Illinois and Iowa, as well as the far-flung places like JFK and London.

Thursday, 15 September 1994

This morning I spent reading Tom Paulin's essay on Yeats 'Meditations in Time of Civil War'. Paulin is always good on the broad view, putting Yeats' timing of publication into perspective. The notion that a writer's decision to *publish* is always a political one, whereas the decision to *write* hardly ever is. In Paulin one can see the flare-up of a trained political mind:

more than mere ideas are at stake when he writes. I suppose this is why he is demanding when it comes to the label 'political poet' – and why he rejected my novel *Without Power* for Field Day. I will always regret the fact that domestic Irish politics is invisible to him. Bred in Ulster, like Seamus Deane, he will never see the serious sociology at work within the Fianna Fáil and Fine Gael parties. Ireland doesn't exist for them unless it intersects with Ulster and the Ulster Crisis. I suppose all my poems and prose about life under the Dáil does frustrate Ulster nationalist intellectuals. It is threatening because I posit in poems and prose a completeness of political activity that distinguishes the two kinds of Ireland. Yet the working out of the Irish bourgeois self-interest, which is at the heart of my prose, does have serious implications for Ulster. Life under the Dáil is attaining a kind of completeness (even in its corruption) that was never arrived at under Stormont. The English didn't corrupt our public life under the Dáil. We corrupted ourselves: this is what really interests me. For example, as a Southern Irish person, I'd like to hear more about embezzlement and how jobs are obtained in Ulster, and not another moan about history. If I could find the corruption I'd believe in Ulster's viability as a culture. The contempt that Ulster Catholics have for life in the Free State is something that fills me with anger. But is it something that Bohemians feel for the Czech Republic, or Alsatians feel for France? Is it the anger of abandonment?

Underlying all Paulin's work is that English Left-trained belief system, the absolute belief in moral standards of discourse. How rotten our Irish political culture is compared to this English decency. It is the difference between Denis Johnston's *The Old Lady Says No* and CP Snow's *Corridors of Power* or *The Conscience of the Rich*.

At what point did our native politics become corrupt? Sometimes it does seem that the whole of the nineteenth century was a nursery of corrupt influence, of intra-Catholic sharp practise. The Catholic nation was robbed in the seventeenth and eighteenth century, no doubt about that. But it could be said that we've spent the first half of the twentieth century paying for the emancipation of Catholic power in the nineteenth century, and that we've spent the second half of the twentieth century paying for the victories of the Land League, the emancipation of the tenant farmer. The beauty of the next century may be that it will bring us the emancipation of the tax-paying consumer. That consumer is the urban Irish Joe Soap who has had to pay for every ounce of freedom won. This is what makes America such a decent place to live: its revolution was begun by citizens angered by unjust taxes, rather than by poets besotted by mystical notions of the nation and the land.

The first teaching week. The English Department like the foyer of the Listowel Arms during Writers' Week. Professors and students with papers and timetables, rushing about. Could you sign this? Can I join your Monday class? I need to do another Senior seminar, could I join yours, Professor please? It is absolutely impossible for me to say no to such pleadings. Now I think my classes will be overloaded. Interesting young writers in the Poetry Workshop: Mike Dawson from an Irish farming community in Northeast Iowa. Names that make their mark: Julie Liu, Debbie Siegel . . .

My office takes on the character of a raft in a stormy ocean. More and more students come in, all in a state of panic, wanting to join my class. Each one has a good excuse, or at least a well-rehearsed one. It is difficult to refuse a place to Seniors who may need a credit for a course in the 'Uppers' as they call it. It's not that they love poetry especially, or poets who write about politics, but they *must* do one more course in my category. So far I have refused no one. If I stayed here for a few years I would develop a thick skin.

I have no doubt about that. I can almost feel that skin forming already.

Saturday, 17 September 1994

At a football match in the Macalester Stadium this evening. Mac played badly, as always. The school has a peculiar pride in its terrible record on the football field. It has a deliberate policy of testing potential footballers academically: in this way it always puts more brain than brawn onto the football field. From the football stand, though, one could see a beautiful Midwestern sunset above the trees. We were really looking downtown over the trees, but the red sky and the huge falling sun made me imagine the great American plain that stretches westwards.

Tuesday, 20 September 1994

Today spent some time reading magazines and books on Ireland. We have been away from Ireland for nearly a month now. Already Ireland begins to form a pattern, it develops a biography. Even its textures and colours begin to organise themselves. This is a dangerous feeling . I don't trust it. The other day I pinned a few photographs of Kerry, Coominole and the 'Ranga', Mount Brandon and Smerwick Harbour, on the noticeboard outside my office. Afterwards I felt that it was not the right thing to do: it was an easy gesture, it said 'Beware. Irish Professor. Special Material.' It is always a mistake to hide behind the mask of one's ethnic background. People here find it hard enough not to say 'Sure-and-begorrah' every time I open my mouth.

Yet what I love most about this English Department is its common humanity. It is very much a community of personal relationships. Today I was talking to a few students about Irish Modernism. They find it difficult to accept that it exists, yet all of them have read Joyce and Beckett. I showed them Coffey's 'Missouri Sequence' and Denis Devlin's 'Lough Derg'. Without much success, I think. They really want more of Kavanagh, more of Heaney, more of the cluttered Irish material. But it is a mistake to *force* them to be modernist, to follow Devlin instead of Heaney. After all, they understand that their own poetry, American poetry, is a broad church, embracing the wildness of Sexton and the formalism of Frost and Lowell. What Devlin and Coffey have in common with Yeats and Heaney is that ability to conserve an achievment centred upon the poem itself, the thing made, and not upon the *idea* of poetry. This is why it's a mistake to tell young poets that they must choose – between an apparent modernism (Devlin, Coffey) and an apparent conservatism (Kavanagh, Heaney). The fact is: the world can rotate around either modernism or conservatism.

It is telling lies to the young – who have not yet had the balancing years of wide reading. In terms of achievement Coffey and Heaney, Joyce and Yeats are one. They respond to the given material of their lives. One should never teach the young to discover 'unIrish' material or 'international' material in order to be more *authentic* as poets. Authenticity is a test that no poet should be subjected to. It is fraught with the corruptions of politics, literary politics. For example, it is not my fault that I was handed Fianna Fáil material when I was a child, any more than it is Joyce's fault that he was handed the material of Clongowes and Ibsen.

Thursday, 22 September 1994

Reading Denis FitzGerald's letter from Glenshelane House. Everything OK in West Waterford, my brother Michael in good form. But DHF says that they've had forty-two inches of rainfall in the garden already this year – more than the whole of last year. I remember a critic complaining that all the rain in *Without Power* was an overworked metaphor. In fact, it wasn't a metaphor at all, it was just the damp reality. Everything growing like mad. Denis says that they are going at everything with saw and grippers instead of hedge-clippers. Good to see his familiar hand-writing, steady and elegant. One of the few steady presences in the engine of my life.

Another hectic day. Three students in conference this morning. A meeting about computers. I don't have a computer in my office. People must think I'm crazy. Even John Bernstein, that lover of everything Florentine and beautiful, admits a computer into his space. In the English Department there's a good computer room – and, more important, a good team of student assistants who love to rescue me from the demands of 'Windows' files. Also, in the Departmental computer room there is a sense of community, a great deal of coming and going. The computer room is more like a kitchen, like the big kitchen at Annaghmakerrig or the kitchen at The Poets' House of Janice Fitzpatrick and James Simmons: people using it are forced into communication at a humane level.

Today we worked on 'Roger Casement' and 'The Ghost of Roger Casement' as well as the Parnell poems and the magnificent 'Municipal Gallery Revisited'. This last poem is a masterful thing, as perfect and contemporary as a Picasso canvas or a Smetana Quartet.

First Papers

Here I pay attention
as I never paid before.
Essays have returned to me
with profligate vengeance;
the pain of attended pages.

Something took my attention
more than thirty years ago.
If only childhood could come back;
the nightmare of Cappoquin,

the insufficient beauty of men
who thinned beet and were silent.
One needs an unbroken father
to bring something to a close.

Young scholars come to my door
wearing roller-blades and Twins caps.
It is their second childhood
I must attend and grade.

Thursday, 29 September 1994

Last class on Yeats. I showed a brief film, an old, well-worn print from the Media Department. Too poetic, too full of atmosphere, with rooks, towers and bogs. This whole Irish thing a bit too much for me. I'd have preferred a film about Saul Bellow or Isaac Bachevis Singer. Something with bite in it. Indeed an interview with Singer would lead to a greater understanding of Yeats than this drivel. Why is it that film people respond to the most trivial, most annoyingly superficial, aspects of a writer's work? So, for Yeats see rooks and towers, for Behan see pubs, for Heaney see bogs ... I long for something that will show the students the excitement, the sheer bloody excitement of Yeats' poetry. Not this tourist rubbish. Then again, some of the most painful scenes in art-house films occur when the director wants to show how intellectuals discuss something at café tables. A film, for impact, has to draw attention to a few dominant preconceptions of the audience. This contrasts with the near absolute freedom of the writer who controls image, audience and idea within the written page. At the end of the day, the impact of a poet is not something visual. Even the visual images are not visual, not meant to be received as painted images but as *ideas* of what is visual.

Saturday, 1 October 1994

One of my favourite places in St Paul is the intersection of Snelling and University Avenues. A huge hyper-market called Rainbow, and the only spot where one can experience something that resembles urban life – many African-Americans, beautiful kids, hassled women, loud music blaring from very run-down American cars. It seems to me that the African-American population retains an incredible loyalty to the US motor industry. To hell with Toyota, they seem to say, give us a decent Yankee car. A great deal of construction work is going on behind this area. I fear it may suffer the fate of improvement. On University, also, a good strip of Asian restaurants.

Tonight we went to the Ordway Music Theatre in downtown St Paul to see Yo Yo Ma, the cellist. The other day I listened to him playing a Bach suite for solo cello on my transistor radio at the office. So much of cultured America comes through to me every day on that ten-dollar radio bought at the hardware store beside Cuppa Joes on Grand. Yo Yo Ma has made the six Bach cello suites his personal dominion.

Reading about him in *The Pioneer Press* and the *Star-Tribune*. Ma was born in Paris to Chinese parents. His family came to America when he was seven years old. He made his public debut at the age of five, overshadowing his older sister Yeou-Cheng who was a gifted violinist. He has a beautiful warm stage presence, a very Irish kind of warmth that you sometimes get from Chinese men. He is quoted in the *Star-Trib*. "A good musician is someone who says: 'How can I contribute?' A musician who says 'I want to be a soloist' is immediately less a musician, because that's not what music is about." Not one of his best concerts, according to John Bernstein who knows his music. But the Elgar piece was extraordinary. Cindy had a great story about the time she worked as a chef: when Ma saw the salad she had arranged he called her an artist. I like that. Being an artist is a matter of temperament: one should be able to recognise the real thing, with a cello or a salad.

Friday, 7 October 1994

What we experience here in Minnesota is not exile. It is more like commuting. It is certainly an insult to our Irish immigrants of the nineteenth century to claim that we suffer the same sense of loss of home, of land, religion and nation. This year I am one of the intellectual commuters, one of the potato-pickers of Academe that includes Montague, Heaney, Muldoon, James Liddy, Seamus Deane ... We know nothing of exile. A generation ago, when poets like James Liddy, Tony Cronin or John Montague journeyed to Iowa, Nebraska and Wisconsin by boat and train, then there must have been some feeling of closeness to the Irish experience in the nineteenth century.

The other day the Poetry and Politics class opened out into a general discussion on immigration and racism. The students were surprised that I felt so much at home in America. Why wouldn't I feel at home? A good deal of American life has been 'formatted' (to use a computer term) so that most Irishmen slot very easily in.

Now, an English person would feel much more at sea in an American environment. What I miss most about being away from Ireland is the absence of English voices. At home in Ireland we are so close to the English. There is just so much traffic, such an exchange of population. English people might think of all the Irish people in Kilburn or Brent, but I think of all the English people who frequent Cork City Library, and the public places of that city. Sometimes all the people borrowing books on a Wednesday morning would have English accents. But then, they may not be English: they could be returned Irish, or second generation Irish from Britain who have gone over to give Ireland a try. The truth is that in Ireland we would be aware of all these ambiguities, all these shades of Englishness and grades of Irishness and Anglo-Irishness. Here, everything is too easily simplified. Socially, Irish people actually like the English. It's impossible to communicate this fact in America. If political commentators would only study the Irish international soccer team – the sociology of that team – they would be able to see the complexity of Ireland's relationship with the English.

But our stay here in Minnesota is not exile. In a shop at Victoria Crossing on Grand Avenue we met a lovely woman whose great-grandfather was a Fenian. She said that there were trunk-fulls of papers in her attic, all about her great-grandfather's exploits as a sea captain on the St Lawrence Seaway. She was almost apologetic about her Fenian ancestors. "The family never discusses this kind of thing," she said, dismissing my barrage of questions. I told her she should get in touch with the Minnesota Historical Society. Too many things get lost in this Eternal Present we all inhabit. But this shopkeeper is typical of one kind of Midwestern Irish-American. The Midwest breeds a healthy kind of amnesia, a smoothing out of ethnic differences. Politeness is the most powerful drug west of Chicago. It is a drug that makes society work well, but this has its drawback for historians and sociologists.

One of the joys of being in America is that for the first time since 1984–85 I can concentrate completely on Catherine.

There are no personal distractions for either of us, no family except our own perfect children, no neglected friends, no enemies: this releases an incredible amount of personal energy within ourselves. This absolutely complete concentration on our love for each other is something that we couldn't have anticipated. For the last month we shared almost every hour of every day. Sometimes Catherine speaks words almost as soon as I think of them. Like today in Napoleon's Café: Catherine spoke about the children, about the football team, about Mike Monahan and Joanne, almost as soon as I had been thinking about them.

Days like this are wonderful; so in tune with each other it is as if our souls were conversing. I suppose this is what it means to be completely and selfishly in love. It isn't of much use to anyone else. I mean it is an inner victory that no one outside of us can even guess at, or take comfort in.

Shower After Lovemaking

Beads of water fall from you
when you move between pine doors.
It is the hour after making love
and the house, with its kettle
singing, its towels crumpled,
allows in the orange light of noon.

I think of the insufficient words
for this day; my fullness of you
as if I had some jurisdiction
or ownership of what is in you.
It is only my own feelings
I possess, but fully, with your

permission. You license the images:
water clings to your beautiful breasts

the way we clung to our lives together
in the years we were not strong.
The day glows like an American cigarette
before us. Your coffee is coming.

Monday, 10 October 1994 — Columbus Day

A day no longer celebrated in America, but passed over in embarrassment, like the 1916 Rising at home. What blessed luck Americans have, that all their revolutionary leaders have never been revised or reviled. They are accepted in the context of their time, and children in grade school learn the basic lessons of greatness from them. In Ireland our own children are being taught by a generation of teachers who are hostile to the history of their own nation. Cynicism, shoneenism and a good deal of coat-trailing are the order of the day in every public domain.

Our tragedy is that the 1798 rebellion failed. If it had succeeded we would have had a Presbyterian-led democracy, very like the American Colonies. But this is to deny the intimacy of Ireland's connection with England. We were never an offshore colony like the Americas. We were always treated like a peninsula, a competing peninsula during the eighteenth century. At the end of the day, the Act of Union was a matter of trade, of stifling Irish competition. It was hardly personal. Not in the way it became personal as a result of so much writing in the nineteenth-century. It took a hundred years before Britain became our personal enemy in the modern sense.

Now they don't know what to teach our children. What is our nation? When did the idea of it die?

The other day we went to a beautiful town north of Stillwater called Taylor Falls. A truly exquisite place of timber-frame houses and elegant trees. A place with no purpose but to sit alone in this world and be beautiful. Visited the Folsom House, the pride and joy of the Taylor Falls Historical Society. The former home of William H Folsom, settler, speculator, lumberman, writer and State Senator. Folsom opened a store in Taylor Falls in 1850, co-founded the Chisago Seminary and co-sponsored the building of the first bridge over the St Croix. In less modest times he would have been made Lord St Croix or the Earl Folsom, rather like Boyle of Lismore. But here in Northwest Minnesota we are in the centre of everything modest and low-Church. That is an essential element of its perfection. The Folsom House on its tree-covered hill stands as a perfect altar of reticence.

We were with Dan and Mary Hardy. Dan, a Republican and organiser of the Minnesota Georgian Society, is an enigmatic Anglophile. Mary, a property auctioneer in St Paul, is an effervescent and lovely Mullingar woman who's lived in Minnesota for twenty years. On the way we stopped off at a pumpkin farm to buy a pumpkin and taste the cinnamon-flavoured hot cider.

Thursday, 13 October 1994

More work today on Auden's social world. I'm not giving the students my best. I know I can teach better than this. It's not that I haven't prepared classes, it's really a matter of paying attention to the students. Are they really getting all these English references? Do they understand the feel of the landscapes? I mean the feel of Auden? I've been trying to get across the idea of Auden's search for a personal landscape. As a poet one of his first agendas was to escape the incoherent wasteland of Eliot. With Auden there is always an attempt at some coherent personal world. Even his provocative praise of industrial parks, factories and failed machinery, is nothing more than the selective personalising of a landscape.

He is closer to Yeats in this. Freud was Auden's Madame Blavatsky. What does it matter if Blavatsky was a fake? She offered Yeats a convenient, bloody-minded alternative to the nineteenth century. The same with Freud: does it matter if he is only a storyteller? Did he not provide a place-lore of the human heart, a kind of *dinnseanchas* of the human condition? And is this not what Auden was after? Poems like 'A Shilling Life' or 'Lay Your Sleeping Head ...' are no less important than the public landscapes of 'Hearing of Harvests' or 'Spain'.

For the next two weeks they will have to look at the *Paris Review* interview as well as MacNeice's *The Strings Are False*. Next week we will read Brian Crozier's and Claud Cockburn's essays from Toynbee's *The Distant Drum*. A hell of a lot of work, for them as well as myself. But there's no way they're getting out of this class without some kind of understanding of the human consequences of a conflict that seemed entirely ideological. The thing is, at a literary level the Thirties conflict was always fought at a vicious personal level. Stalin was always personal. Historians tend to forget that. Poets can never forget it. Later, when we do the raw sequences like 'Triptych' in Heaney's *Field Work*, they will see what I am looking for.

Saturday, 15 October 1994

We took a paddle-steamer on the Mississippi River. As the boat churned through the water I felt a terrific sense of unreality. A tedious journey, despite everything. I hate things that move slowly. Nothing in the world outside books is so compelling that one has to move forward at only five miles an hour. I made up for the slow motion of the paddle-steamer by chasing Neil upstairs and downstairs from the inner saloon to the outer deck. We moved imperiously up and down the Mississippi through a ruined Audenesque landscape. It was interesting to approach the St Anthony Falls, the original settlement of

Minneapolis. The journey wasn't as interesting as say, a quick spin down the Naas dual carriageway. To be honest, after our visits to Stillwater and Taylor Falls, it is difficult to be impressed by anything else in Minnesota.

Monday, 17 October 1994

Very cold. Walked to SuperAmerica on St Clair to get a bar of chocolate and drinks for the kids. Also, to clear my head after tonight's poetry workshop. My head not so much cleared as anaesthetised by the chilling still air. It is lovely to walk up St Clair towards Mississippi River Boulevard on nights like this. During the day the College is like any busy place, but at night the whole place takes on a distinctive American neighbourhood atmosphere.

Two highway patrol cars were parked at the filling-station. Three cops chatting beside the coffee machine, their radios crackling, their coffee cups steaming. A young Asian behind the counter. Korean, impeccably dressed and efficient. He breaks into a smile when he sees me. I am one of his late-evening regulars. We chat about the weather in a very un-American way. I think it is a comfort to both of us. At this time of the day America is overwhelming. There is really very little else. The non-American world doesn't even seem like a possibility until the early morning when Public Radio rebroadcasts the BBC World Service and *The New York Times* confirms Europe's existence in its news reports.

The Monday poetry workshop is difficult. The time of the class, 7 p.m. to 10 p.m., may have something to do with this. I am a morning person, not an evening worker. After 8 o'clock my energy is gone. Completely. I thought the workshop would be easy. It's not that the students are bad. There are good writers, like Thea Gelbspan, Debbie Siegel, Keith Bloomgarden, and the stylish duo, Bea Westigard and Alicia

Kunkel. But I cannot get them to adopt some European element of rudeness and bad manners. They are so courteous to each other that the workshop deteriorates into gaps of silence. I can't understand why young writers would allow a gap in conversation. I long for the angry banter of Listowel, four savage poets speaking together, shouting as if poetry was vital to their lives. But not this exhausting courtesy. Maybe they can't quite get the measure of me, and this prevents them from being open. I wonder does Al Greenberg have these kind of silences? I must talk to him. I am very conscious that I may have inherited a well established pattern of work, especially among the Juniors and Seniors (Third and Fourth Years). And why would these young writers want to adopt my style of exchange and banter when they'd have to return to Al Greenberg's style next year? I can't help longing for some student to say "Your poem is *fuckin'* terrible". Somehow, to hear that register of personal rage, to insist on the excellence of the poem, is a matter of life and death for me. Especially when I'm in a good mood.

Thursday, 20 October 1994

We went to downtown Minneapolis with Cindy to see the new frescoes painted on the ceiling of the College of St Thomas business campus. A great party, mighty crowds. I dunno about the frescoes. We live in a world that hates allegory. Allegory can't survive multi-culturalism: it's impact is based upon shared moralities and world views. There is really nothing as morally narrow as an entire wall painted over. Just look at the murals of Ulster housing projects.

Monday, 24 October 1994

A great full-page report by Mindy Aloff in today's *New York Times* about the New York Transit Authority's 'Poetry in Motion'. Riders of the D-train are being asked to contemplate Emily Dickinson and Sir Walter Raleigh. Lorca's 'Ode to Walt Whitman', translated by Ben Belitt, has been placed in 5,900 trains and 3,700 buses:

> *'Ah, filthy New York,*
> *New York of cables and death.*
> *What angel do you carry, concealed in your cheek?'*

As Aloff says: 'Poets need New York: it's a first-rate graduate school for moral indignation.'

Tuesday, 25 October 1994

Today was a truly wasted day. In class we worked on Auden's interview with *The Paris Review* as well as the aphorisms. I tried to get volunteers to read Spender's *World Within World* so that we could have a general discussion on the mind-set of an educated English liberal. There were no takers, but much avoidance of the Professor's eyes. Fall break is upon us, and with it comes a sense of fatigue among students, as real as famine fever among the inmates of Skibbereen Workhouse. Their fatigue gave me a curious license, so that I spent most of the afternoon reading a brilliant memoir of St Paul, *A Romantic Education*, by Patricia Hampl. I bought it the other day in a used bookstore across the street from Macalester – the same building where Richard Ryan, the Irish poet and Ambassador, survived a Minnesota winter while teaching at St Thomas when Eoin McKiernan was Chair of that English Department. All of these connections. The book, though, gorgeous, insightful, lyrical with lyrical feelings (like O'Connor's *Only Child*), and a treasure-trove of sensations from bus journeys around St Paul. I read 120 pages in a single sitting. One of those books that grab the heart. I put the book down at the point where she waves farewell to a fascinating undergraduate at the University of Minnesota, a young woman who would become a model in Paris:

> She waved gaily from the curb as I, a lit face in a darkened rectangle, passed down St Clair Avenue towards home.

There is another city in the book, Prague. The most beautiful city in Europe. *Zlata Praha*, the city of her grandmother. I flicked through the other 180 pages, impatient, wanting to consume the whole thing. But it's a treat that waits in store for me.

Wednesday, 26 October 1994

Talking with Catherine is one of the best things about America. Why can't we have this kind of time at home in Ireland? Do all college professors in Ireland have this kind opportunity to talk to the people in their lives? It's not that I don't work hard. I do. But for the first time in twenty years I feel I have power to manage each day. Today, long chats at Napoleon's Café. The other day, we were chatting so much that three hours went by. It was time to collect the kids from Groveland. Panic. But the happy panic that people have when they know that their time idled away was a deep time.

Friday, 28 October 1994

The terrible political seriousness of Charles Donnelly and John Cornford. Spender, at least, honours Cornford at every turn.

Donnelly, a Co Tyrone man, was part of the Connolly Column which in turn was part of the Lincoln Brigade. He died on the Jarama Front in February 1937. In his 'Poem', he actually defines the difference between the professional poet and the poet of action. What defines them both is 'simple action'. Only the moment of commitment, what he honestly describes as 'Simple and unclear moment', only that moment divides the two kinds of poet.

I wonder if this is enough, if this definition is sufficiently strong to affect the best students? Donnelly was no fool. In many ways he reminds me of Austin Clarke who was to fight his own private Spanish Civil War with the Francos of Irish life. How like Clarke this sounds:

> Your flag is public over granite. Gulls fly above it.
> Whatever the issue of the battle is, your memory
> Is public, for them to pull awry with crooked hands ...

('Poem')

It is the moral reticence of Donnelly that makes him interesting. Sacrifice has not spent all his intellectual resources. He challenges Auden in a way that Pearse could never challenge Yeats or Bobby Sands challenge Heaney. It is a question of the level of discourse. Donnelly's education allows him to operate at the level of Auden or MacNeice. Berrigan never reaches the level of Lowell, despite his sophistication. Norman Mailer, when he writes about anti-War readings, writes it all up as an orchestra of personal styles. Donnelly is interesting in that he challenges his own poetic material, not just at the level of poem-making but at the level of ideology.

Sunday, 30 October 1994 — Halloween

Without doubt, this was one of the most magic nights we've spent since coming to America. Kate and Neil, dressed up as a witch and Power Ranger, did the rounds of houses in Vernon Street and Macalester Street to mark Halloween. (Last night they'd gone to a Zoo Boo at Como Zoo, a hugely well-attended fund-raiser.) Catherine took them into the Macalester College houses of residence where the students put on a brilliant show for all the kids. But it was on the streets that American adults showed just how wonderful they were: porches and drives hung with lanterns and masks, fairy lights, chimes and flickering candles. People who came to the door to give treats were often dressed up themselves, entering completely into the spirit of things.

At the end of the evening we all called to Coach Bell and Maureen, and to Dorothy Baeur, our indefatigable ninety-year old neighbour. An extraordinary evening.

Tuesday, 1 November 1994

The days turning colder. Winter's Minnesotan needle gradually inserted into our consciousness. When the snow comes we will have already gone under this anaesthetic of the cold.

Thursday, 3 November 1994

Catherine's birthday. We went to a brilliant restaurant, *Chez Colette*, with John and Cindy. But first, to 219 Vernon Street for champagne.

Tuesday, 8 November 1994

A disastrous election night for the Democrats. Ann Wynia threw away the election for Governor of Minnesota, with the help of almost every socialist and gay supporter of the Democratic party. The liberals betrayed Clinton with a well-rehearsed chorus of extremist fringe interventions at almost every public opportunity. Even before the night was lost, a weird youth, who was obviously high on something, appeared as a spokesperson for the Minneapolis Democrats. No Party discipline, a desperate fear of upsetting the wild Left elements at the very moment when such discipline would have galvanised the support of conservative Clinton followers. The Wynia campaign was like watching the best and brightest commit group suicide. Or like watching the Irish Labour Party in action.

Went with Nick Coleman to a few polling stations in the neighbourhood. As the local votes began to tally I could see the truth dawning. By the time we went to Congressman Bruce Vento's party in a palatial mansion the pennies were already rolling in: one group was having a hostile encounter with another. The blame was being apportioned over the wine and cheese. We drove to downtown Minneapolis where another party that was more like a state funeral was taking place. Everybody saying that Clinton is a disaster, a President who has betrayed every liberal promise. *Plus ça change*.

People need to vent their anger, I suppose. And it is easy for an outsider to understand what's happened. It doesn't require an Einstein to figure it out. The Republicans played one big right-wing game with the electorate, while the Democrats played lots of little games as if political power was a kind of undergraduate seminar. I tried to keep my mouth shut. This isn't my country. But, you know, I've developed a fondness if not a love for this state. Still, I said so much, too much, I was lucky to be offered a lift home across the Mississippi to this quiet corner of St Paul.

The lights of the St Clair Broiler still blinking at 2 a.m. One expects Dashell Hammett or Raymond Chandler to emerge from its lobby. Eternal America.

And, in the distance, the sound of a train coming up over the bluffs. At this time of night it could be *The Empire Builder* en route to Chicago. What a disaster for the Democrats. It's true that, given only one bullet, an elector would shoot a liberal on a high horse instead of a conservative evading tax.

In a democracy the ballot paper is that habitual one bullet.

Friday, 11 November 1994

This evening I actually wore a white shirt and a good tie. The Class of 1995 held their Senior Social in the Wayerheuser Lounge. A party in the company board-room. An important right of passage that the Seniors take seriously. Good jazz and trad. Saw a few of my students, elegantly dressed and not too drunk. As I left the lounge I looked back. A small group, the expert party-goers of the future, had gathered into a circle. A bright glow of contentment from their table. Good luck to them.

Tuesday, 15 November 1994

A long conversation with Tom Redshaw on the phone about Nuala Ní Dhomhnaill's poetry. Tom is trying to come to terms with the Muldoon translations; alarmed, I think, by the literal meanings and the Muldoon 'equivalences' in the English language. I often wonder myself about those texts, but I've probably less Irish than Muldoon who lived in the Kerry

Gaeltacht after he left the BBC in Belfast. There is pure and simple mischief in some of the translations:

> *Tagann an traein dubh*
> *isteach sa staisiún*

becomes, in Muldoon,

> *As surely as the Headless Horseman*
> *came to Ichabod Crane.*

Why does he link the Black Train with 'The Legend of Sleepy Hollow' by Washington Irving? Then again, he does something like turning *bordálann siad/an traein cheanna* into 'they all will mount/ the gangway of the Windigo'. This appears to be self-indulgent Muldoon until one realises that the word 'gangway' is like the German word *ausgang* or 'exit'. At the end of this poem there are cattle-wagons, Dachau and Belson. None of these words are in the original. What Muldoon is doing is spectacular: he is creating a third text, not a version in English. But this third text, neither Muldoon or Ní Dhómhnaill, is probably closer to the subliminal, voyage of the psyche stuff that Nuala has been creating in Irish. It's not a question of knowing Irish. It's really a question of knowing how a poem creates its distinctive signature.

I think of that entry in Seferis' journal where he writes about Rex Warner whom he had asked to translate *The King of Asine*. Seferis had been warned by colleagues that Warner didn't have much Greek. But what mattered to Seferis was Warner's command of his own language.

In the same way, one couldn't say that Waley or Pound betrayed Chinese poets with their versions. The versions are all the more interesting because the originals are ultimately untranslatable.

A good deal of Ní Dhómhnaill's work is beyond translation. Her bravado alone is something that belongs to the Irish literary world, and only that world. The Anglophone world deadens certain things that are in Irish, in the same way that the English language betrayed Freud by making a false scientific language out of his very down-to-earth German words.

It's difficult to be pushy and sexy in that *díreach* way that Ní Dhomhnaill has in Irish. Just as it's difficult to get at the spirit of 'Midnight Court' or at the full impact of Maire Mhac an tSaoi's '*Ceathrúinti Mháire Ní Ogáin*'. It's not that the feelings are quaint, it's just that they are so advanced in terms of subject matter and demands on the reader. Nearly thirty years ago Mhac an tSaoi could write a feminist text like '*Cré na Mná Tí*', seven exquisite lines about being a housewife and an artist:

> *Ach, ar nós Sheicheiriseaide,*
> *Ní mor duit an fhilíocht chomh maith.*

When Eavan Boland tried to say the same things in English, in *In Her Own Image*, she was slated by the critics. This tells us a great deal about the conservatism of English language thought in Irish poetry. In many ways, both during the Second World War and immediately afterwards, Irish language poets connected with everything that was modern, existentialist and French. What amazes me is that the Irish language seems insulated from the material of Ireland: the gap between Kavanagh and Eluard seems immense, but there is no distance between Ó Ríordáin or Arland Ussher and Eluard. It seems to me that these Irish language poets were using the contraceptive of European thought long before it was legal in our Republic. Hence, the appropriateness of Muldoon. His sensibility is as modernist as these new Gaelic poets.

Tuesday, 15 November 1994 (later that day)

Two weeks of Lowell. Difficult to isolate *Notebook* in the way
I had hoped. One can't talk about the political Lowell without
reading the two early worlds of religion and family. With
Lowell America is personal. For Mary McCarthy, Daniel
Berrigan, Bob Dylan, Denise Levertov and others, the Vietnam
conflict was an issue of political and moral dishonour. When
Lowell thinks of a US gunboat off the coast of Vietnam, it's
Commander Lowell he wants to tell to get the hell out of there.
America is more than a country: it is personal in a Yeatsean
way. Norman Mailer in *Armies of the Night* does create a kind
of family argument out of the community of writers, in the
same way that Lowell creates a family afternoon out of the
history of America. Mailer, surprisingly, sells himself short. He
succumbs to Lowell's fame in a very unhealthy way. He
shouldn't have been so impressed. He is Mailer, after all. Still,
those are magic sonnets: 'For Robert Kennedy', 'For Eugene
McCarthy', and the utterly brilliant 'Mexico'. Was there ever an
Irish writer who could write in such an understated manner in
such a blaze of self confidence? Probably Heaney, in the years
after *Field Work*, or Kinsella during the early Seventies. The
other day I read to the students from Heaney's 'Lowell's
Command' in *The Government of the Tongue*. Some of them
could see the connection between both poets.

After class a few students came with me as far as Cuppa
Joes on Grand. A lively discussion on poets and politics. The
world has changed. Sometimes I think that being political goes
against the grain of everyone under the age of thirty. But I
must be wrong. I must be. The energy of politics can't have
fled completely from English Departments to Sociology
Departments. Students nowadays have such a keen sense of
their own private lives that nothing vital is ceded in the
common room or seminar room. Will this intensification of
private life lead to a new kind of poetry, a poetry of ellipsis

rather than a poetry of commitment? Perhaps in every era there is only so much political IQ available in English Departments. Nowadays, ninety per cent of the available IQ is used up in Women's Studies. The brightest students end up in that discipline: it offers the greatest challenge to a really intellectual youngster.

Friday, 18 November 1994

At a book launch in the University Club at Summit Avenue. I drove there in our Dodge Omni, braving St Paul traffic for a few hundred yards. I overshot the Club and almost got lost in the dark streets while trying to turn around. I felt like a character in a Scott Fitzgerald novel as I wandered through the foyer of the warm Victorian building. A mighty crowd had assembled to hear the Hon. Desmond Guinness and Jacqueline O'Brien talking about Dublin's Georgian architecture. They were promoting an excellent and lavish book on Dublin's interiors. The whole do sponsored by Dan and Mary Hardy, Minnesota's Irish Georgians. Desmond and Jacqueline both very giddy, and full of good humoured mischief. For part of the talk the slides were shown upside down. "Oh, go on, they're only ceilings," Desmond Guinness replied in a wicked, tipsy voice when someone pointed out the error. I left early, worried about the route home.

While walking to the car I met a man who said he'd come to St Paul from Wisconsin to find a cure for his alcoholism. He was attending a day-care clinic in the Twin Cities. He asked me if I'd come with him for a cup of coffee at Victoria Crossing. There were so many things that he understood about himself now, he said. It would be good to talk to an Irishman about alcohol and about his victory over the disease. He kept using the word 'victory' as if it were a personal pronoun. (The way Ian Paisley uses the word 'outrage'.) I was too worried about driving back up Summit Avenue to accompany him for a coffee. Also, he carried a very large yellow-handled scissors in his hand. I told him he should go into the University Club out of the cold, to say at the door that he was with the Irish Georgian Society. He stared at me as if I had two heads, but he turned back and headed up towards the Club. I wished him well. I felt that I'd encountered the ghost of F Scott Fitzgerald.

Sunday, 20 November 1994

Yesterday, an early morning flight to Milwaukee to read to James Liddy's group during an Irish Festival. Marvellous crowd, terrific response. Felt almost as positive as Desmond Guinness. Milwaukee must have one of the most civilised airports in the US In the airport terminal, one of the best used-bookstores I've seen in years. Editions of Yeats, Joyce, Hemingway, Robert Penn Warren. I could have spent the day browsing happily, but James Liddy discovered me leafing through a copy of Gide's *Journals*. I was reading that entry, at the beginning of the Great War, when the cat knocks over a Meissen vase. At that moment Gide thought it an appropriate image for what lay in store for Europe during the twentieth century. Liddy, eloquent, erudite, welcoming, charming. A poet who has made his own niche and lived there authentically, from the heady Dublin days of *Arena* to the quiet academe of Milwaukee. It was wonderful to spend a day in such an intensely Irish atmosphere, and with companions who might, at any moment, be ruined by the material of our native land. This is how serious a life in literature should be.

Sunday, 27 November 1994

Sunday after Thanksgiving. Snow began to fall this morning. I drove up St Clair in the falling snow to SuperAmerica to buy the *New York Times* and the *Pioneer Press*. I came back covered in snow, but as happy and ennervated as Minnesotans are by the first serious sight of winter. After the first snowfall Minnesota's production rate goes way up. Investors invest more, workers work more, poets write more. Politicians become more honest. Each resident of Minnesota, Irish or African-American, Korean or Hmung, becomes Scandanavian and serious for the duration of the snow.

But today's snow was entirely personal. Kate and Neil are wild with excitement. They can't believe that the snow goes on and on. After a few hours I began to clear the path and steps to the house. I was the only adult outdoors. Dorothy our neighbour came to her door to give me an important lesson on the etiquette of snow. "Did you not listen to the weather forecast, dear? There's no point clearing the snow away. This will go on for another twelve hours." I went indoors sheepishly, trying to cover my yard brush with my coat as I ascended the steps. God forbid that anyone should see an idiot sweeping snow in the middle of a snowstorm. Kate and Neil playing in the snow, running and jumping, shouting and laughing, were much more in tune with what the afternoon required.

These have been wonderful days, these free days of Thanksgiving. That is, after the exhaustion of teaching. I had no idea how much pressure college professors cope with. Now I know. The more intelligent the students, the greater the pressure. Teaching is so dangerous for writers and artists. Teaching squats on one's head, occupying all those cerebral spaces that rightly belong to the making of poems and novels.

I stay indoors, brewing tea and reading the papers. Yet another excellent feature in the *New York Times* about poetry in the business world. It focuses on John Barr, the new President of the Poetry Society of America and Ted Kooser, the brilliant poet who has worked in insurance for thirty years.

John Barr says he wakes at 3 a.m. and spends a few hours on his poetry. His day job is in New York as a partner with utility financial advisors, Barr Devlin Associates. In this feature, a great photograph of Barr looking out of his Manhattan office window. Dana Gioia, who was once a vice-president at Kraft Foods is quoted: "Many writers have made careers in business because of the career uncertainties of the arts world." Only a few days ago I was reading Gioia's collection *The Gods of Winter* from Graywolf Press in St Paul. The paper quotes Ted Kooser's lovely poem, 'Tom Ball's Barn':

> *The loan that built the barn*
> *just wasn't big enough*
> *to buy the paint, so the barn*
> *went bare and fell apart*

It seems to tell the story of my life. All of Kooser is like that, wise in a Robert Frost-like way. Kooser, in his mid-fifties now, works for Lincoln Benefit Life in Nebraska – but as always, there's more to any poet than the workplace. Kooser, for example, studied with Karl Shapiro at Iowa State. Later, two paragraphs on, a poet who lives as a verse writer for Hallmark Cards. This is Barbara Loots who says: "I've been with Hallmark for twenty eight years. Hallmark has a culture that nourishes me more than an academic culture would."

She's a brave woman.

I get up from the Sunday papers and look out the window. It's still snowing and it's 9 p.m.

Monday, 28 November 1994

Everywhere on campus, the sound of snow-blowers and snow being blown skywards into ditches and over walls. A thrill to walk in the snow and to see the street lights and garden lights of Macalester Drive and the rear of Vernon Street, everything softer, like gaslight, in the evening snow. The blueness of everything, even newspapers in corner newstands. The disappearance of animals. No dogs in yards, and where have all the squirrels gone?

This morning Catherine was reading a *Sunday Tribune* sent from home by Tadhg Coakley. She quotes Joe O'Connor. From this distance his dissent is familiarising and comforting. Peculiar how our lives are affected by columnists. At home one is constantly annoyed, vindicated, outraged, encouraged, by columnists like Fintan O'Toole, Nuala O'Faolain. Catherine's mother, Kitty, sent us a gift subscription of the Saturday *Irish Times*. On Tuesday I noticed the *Irish Independent* is now for sale in The Hungry Mind Bookstore. At five thousand miles we hang onto the words of columnists, reading them again and again. Even their protests against Irish life become a deep connection with home.

This is why exile is such a suspect state of being. It softens the brain. What kind of drop in standards has occurred when one can name Nuala O'Faolain and Shane Ross in the same breath; when one can see them as equal objects of affection? This is not right. In truth those who are exiled can speak accurately of nothing except the true sense of being exiled. Being out of Ireland is truly awful if one is trying to understand it or teach its material. There is nothing especially intelligent or important about Ireland, but it is a distinctive place. And exile from it separates one from the lucidity of its very real madness.

Wednesday, 30 November 1994

Twenty essays on my table, uncorrected. Elizabeth Bowen's *Last September* and Neil Jordan's *The Past*, with all their scraps of papers and folded notes, in my bag to be read carefully for next semester's Senior seminar. The work mounts up. Today I feel overwhelmed by all the preparations still to be completed. Really looking forward to the January break and our journeys to New York and Vermont.

Monday, 5 December 1994

Just graded twenty exam papers on Robert Lowell. Two or three exceptional readings of what we studied in class. I have given out too many A grades.

I can feel the semester not closing but falling apart. I haven't written a good poem for over a year. Under my table in the English Department is a Roches Stores bag full of notes for my third and final Party novel. Maybe in Spring I'll get a chance to work on it. But right now I've lost my Minnesotan energy level.

Thursday, 8 December 1994

Tackling Heaney. Despite the nearness of his fame and my own feel for the material, it's difficult to know if the class understands anything of this material. One can see immediately that Heaney had his own personal vocabulary.

Spent today reading 'Singing School' from *North*. It's an anthology of Heaney's various styles. Parts 2 and 3 are early Heaney, with all the gurgling and cocky sounds. Part 6, though, is a different kettle of fish – lucid, tight, defeated, but defeated in the way the human heart is defeated. It would be interesting to compare this sequence and 'Tryptch', (from *Field Work*) with Seferis's 'Thrush' sequence from the mid-Forties. All of these poems come at a point of political decline and resolution. (That is, political decline within the poet's imaginative life. The irony here is that this decline in a set of moral beliefs often comes at a point of renewed personal strength.) In this sense a writer like Gerry Adams (fiction) or Bobby Sands (poetry) reaches for art at their point of greatest weakness. What I'm waiting for is someone who'll attack this problem in an essay. Neither Seferis nor Heaney expect too much from their art. Adams and Sands expect to be redeemed by it in their unequal struggle with the British. Their expectations ruin the very basis of their writing. Not a matter of feeling pain, but of expressing the pain well. No active revolutionary would accept this distinction. But an artist knows it to be true. It's the very thing that makes writing well worth the bother.

Friday, 9 December 1994

While I was in my office a phone-call from The Hungry Mind Bookstore to let me know that the copies of *Dubliners* had come into stock for next semester's seminar. I went down after class to collect my desk copy. Took it back to the student grill where I had a coffee and read Terence Brown's Introduction. Brown, a socialist manqué in the way I'm a FF-manqué, gets to grips immediately with the social setting of the stories. He sees Dublin society, or the Joycean part of it, as a paralysed place – where the height of social advancement is to have made a fortune in the grocery trade supplying RIC Barracks. The idea, also, that Joyce has given us a book of churches in a community without true grace. Also, Brown cautions against reductive, simplistic readings of the collection; and advances the idea that Joyce's use of the symbolic is more akin to the humane method of Flaubert than the trembling veils of Symons or Yeats.

I had come to the end of 'A Mother', page 148 of the Brown edition, by the time I'd lifted my head. Damn blast it, a conference with a student missed, a Sophomore who wants to spend his Junior year in Ireland. When I got back to the office I found a note pinned to the door, with just one word:

'Professor?'

That question mark was rather cheeky. But very Macalester. Very stylish.

Full of Joycean feelings (a kind of viral infection that Colbert Kearney used to warn undergraduates at UCC against), I wrote this:

Bigger than the Liffey

You know the way chalk breaks like a hostile editor
or the way chairs form a ring – around the word
paralysis, for instance. You scratch at the heart for
some intuit meaning. Meaning is the card
pinned to crepe paper. Meaning is the theatre,
the candlesticks carried upstairs;
a child, an old woman's head at the banister,
even the personal odour of cut flowers.
It could be worse. You could be back
beside a river bigger than the Liffey.
Childhood: as far as one can go from where ideas form.
You could be a child watching the chalice crack,
wondering who broke Christ's decanter of sherry –
whether the world is mortal, venial or only a gnomon.

The above is the kind of thing that Colbert Kearney wanted to nip in the bud: earnest young scholars inspired to respond in the Joycean manner. I wonder if anyone will emerge from Joyce at next year's seminar? I doubt if any of my students were educated by Jesuits. Benedictines, maybe. But not Jesuits.

Saturday, 10 December 1994

Looking at the calendar for next year. Spring break is March 18-26. The mid-term grades are due March 29. All classes end by May 12, with Commencement on May 20. My appointment ends officially in the middle of June, after which time we will merely be trespassing in America. Strange feeling today. It must be my reading of the Joyce stories: I thought for the first time about going home to Cork. The prospect didn't seem too terrible. Reading Elizabeth Bowen, of course, makes me think of the landscape of the Blackwater, Mallow and Kildorrery – Catherine's country that I love twice over because of my love for her.

Monday, 12 December 1994

My last Poetry Workshop, ended at 10.20 p.m. Walked home on a very cold night, exhausted and perplexed. Did they get anything out of this workshop? I don't think I dominated it enough, or encouraged my own style of exchange: I let them engage with each other in the way they were used to. I should have created a greater spark. Two of the students came back to thank me. Perhaps we are all too tired. No sense of occasion. This kind of parting saddens me. This workshop was not a success. I couldn't get a sense of continuing improvement. I didn't get to know the students well enough. There were too many people in the class. Sometimes I counted twenty-five people sitting round the room: ten too many. If ever I do a College writing workshop again I will restrict the number to twelve or fourteen.

Tuesday, 13 December 1994

A reception at Michael Keenan's house on Ashland Avenue. Michael, Chair of the English Department, and his wife, Susan are retiring soon. They've already bought a house in New Mexico, in a beautiful, burned landscape like Spain or the Greek islands. Michael bucking against the traces, longing to go. The traffic on Summit Avenue very heavy, but Ashland is a quieter oasis.

Still waiting on a few portfolios of poems from my Monday night poetry class. Ana Troncoso today. Alicia Kunkel given until 4 p.m. next Monday. After that we will be gone. In New York, with Greg Delanty's brother, Norman, the brain physician, and his wife, Breda. Then to Vermont for Christmas.

Wednesday, 14 December 1994

Reading poems and grading. And reading, yet again, *The Last September*, one of the most perfect Irish novels. There are so many layers in this, our only Bloomsbury political novel. The material of Ireland was one way that Bowen escaped from the domination of Virginia Woolf. Ireland differentiates her talent from everything else in Bloomsbury; in the way Ireland serves to detach Louis MacNeice from the over-bearing influence of Auden. Ireland, in this sense, although a tragedy, is actually a technical advantage.

The character of Lois is pure Bloomsbury, like many of the supercilious characters in her early stories in *Encounters*. They live between worlds, constantly becoming something or someone, but then backing off. Coming back and forth from the lighthouse of adulthood or art. Bowen uses phrases like 'an emotional kind of straying' or 'startled into beauty' And that sense of the life in things: a room responds, a house sleeps, a wicker-chair discusses someone after they sit in it.

This could have been yet another sub-Virginia Woolf novel or Louis MacNeice poem. So what does Bowen do? She makes an IRA man break cover in front of her young sensitive heroine:

Here was something else she could not share. She could not conceive of her country emotionally: it was a way of living, an abstract of several landscapes, or an oblique frayed island, moored at the north but with an air of being detached and washed out west from the British coast.

The destiny of Lois and Sir Richard and Lady Naylor is tested against the War of Independence. Sir Richard's gestures and speeches are brilliant. He hates the 'jolly old army of occupation' (the Hartigans' phrase) because it introduces conflicts that damage his own deep relationships with the native Irish. The impersonality of the conflict offends him. The whole thing brilliantly constructed by Bowen. Maybe not as much depth as Joyce, but easily as much political savvy.

Friday, 23 December 1994

New York. Noisy, intense, the signature of Irish life in every street. At night, the great rumble of the monster: wealth and work, never sleeping. Norman Delanty's apartment is across the street from the Cornell Medical Centre. Thirty floors up. Breakfast this morning at Neil's Diner on the corner of Seventy-First and Lexington. To the zoo at Central Park. Withdrew some cash from an ATM machine at Citibank on First Avenue. Not that we needed the money, but just to be part of my first New York queue. Now I can feel like a New Yorker. Almost immediately upon arrival I fantasise about coming back here for a week, just with Catherine, to take in more bookstores and museums. Kate and Neil love it. The zoo and FAO Schwartz. It's absurd to think one could take in anything useful in just three days.

Monday, 26 December 1994 — St Stephen's Day

A quiet Christmas at Greg Delanty's in Vermont. Extremely cold when the sun goes down. We came here in a small commuter aircraft that trundled along like a hay cart on the Mount Melleray Road.

Greg's company a tonic, but we keep losing him. Gone yesterday, then today he plans to head off to San Diego to an MLA conference. As a poet in America now he needs to go to conferences for his career. As I'm heading back to Cork City Library I have respect for these promotional journeys. Being a young writer in the academic world is a constant struggle. There is a whole world of MLAs, conferences, seminars to which I've never been privy. Working in a library I've had that luxury of laziness, inertia. When Greg's around I can see my own damning inertia. I don't write to people, I don't answer letters, I don't make phone calls. I think I am a hermit. Catherine and the children are not feeling well after picking up a bug in New York.

On the radio I hear that John Osborne has died. What an obnoxious man he was: his anger was never quite enough. Greg and I have a good bitch about him. Not that he ever did anything to us or to anyone we knew. But it sharpens our knives before we get down to discussing Irish writers.

Despite Greg's restlessness, I get a strong feeling of benevolence from his company – it's as if life, and the literary life especially, were a kind of beach on a summer evening from which one never wants to be called away. How can us poets of the South ever be taken seriously if we laugh so much together? Cork City especially is a place that's underestimated by outsiders because they see so much tomfoolery and laughter. We have no great theme, no national theme, like the Ulster poets: nothing that might alter the destiny of our land. But O'Connor, O'Faolain and Ó Ríordáin do show us that we have the great theme of ourselves. The foul rag-and-bone shop of our foul rag-and-bone shop.

There's nothing in our Province that might be a metaphor. But it is the Province of Spenser, Raleigh and Merriman. We must be able to do something with it. It is true that we drank and gossiped right through the Ulster crisis. For this, history will be our harsh judge.

There is a distinct rhythm in the gossip and the laughter of Cork; it sparkles through Greg, the poet. It is a powerful thing, Cork, if only it could be caught in poetry the way Bowen caught it in her prose. Staying with Greg reminds me how much I love Cork City, especially my own personal part, the neo-classical ancient heart of Montenotte with its windy, draughty windows and bramble-covered high walls. There's nothing like it anywhere, for sheer bloody-mindedness of style. Even here in Vermont I can feel Cork's crippling self-absorbed music. When I go home I must pay attention to this.

Saturday, 31 December 1994

Catherine has gone with Kate and Neil to see the old Vanderbilt farm near Sherbourne on Lake Champlain. I've been reading another book on the Twin Cities; *French Lessons* by Alice Kaplan, a Professor of French at Duke University. Wonderful descriptions of upper middle-class life in the Mid-West. Summers on Lake Minnetonka and school in Switzerland. Then the encounters with France and things French, from 'Andre', her lover, to the narrator of Patrick Modiano's *Remise de peine*. Lovely, stylish memory and so much pain of a really French kind. This extraordinary American capacity to suffer like others.

Spent hours with this book, the same kind of hours I spent with Patricia Hampl's memories. Listening to one of Greg's tapes of Chopin's nocturnes. The stern reflective nature of the music, the quiet imprisonment of an apartment in December Vermont. Ultimately, this is what words do, whether poetry or prose, in Paris or Prague. They allow us to absorb woeful things that have happened.

Yesterday we drove to the ski resort of Stowe in the Mansfield Mountain area. A place of breath-taking beauty with sheer rock faces and 4,000 foot ski runs. We took a gondola to the top of one mountain and stopped at a cliff-top restaurant. A strange place, elegant because of the snow. What is it about ski resorts? In our culture they mean Hemingway skiing to a railway station or James Bond slipping through pine forests, or Brigitte Bardot in a Roger Vadim film. A place to write a novel, fall in love, plan a film or make a poem.

I sat at the table and thought about our coming to America. A good decision. To see a land far more complex and troubled than our own. In our own land there is one major problem left for us to solve; in America there are huge problems to be solved simultaneously. This years I've seen Kate and Neil cope with a milieu very different from the neighbourhoods of Cork. But to be here with Catherine, all of this has been a gift.

But in my office in Minnesota are all the jumbled chapters of the third and final Party novel. It is difficult to work on the third one when the other two have been remaindered. I feel utterly betrayed by that act of Poolbeg Press. But I'm determined that 1995 will see the completion, however flawed and however unsung, of the Glenville Trilogy. In its pages I'll put everything that I imagine a political childhood might be. The Party was such a narrow part of my childhood, beginning at the age of nine or ten with John Fraher of Cappoquin and ending in my late teens. But the Party has been a causeway for me across all the boggy regions of my life. At the time I never saw Fianna Fáil as any kind of failure. It was only when I went to College that the Party became for me a kind of failed father. But the failed father is my earlier self, my unliterary self. I feel Alice Kaplan or Patricia Hampl would understand this.

However, this day belongs to Vermont. The renewing fall of snow that makes me worry about Catherine and the kids who are still out on the snow-covered roads. The Chopin seems to go on and on. In the end, it is all a form of music. Life, I mean, it is a repeating melody that we overhear, coming from far away. It always seems to come from the faraway lives of others, but, of course, it is really just our own personal music that we can hear when it returns to us. Snow falls against the almost opaque double-windows of this Burlington apartment. It has a kind of impersonal melancholy. Coming from Ireland, I know I worry too much about the dangers of ice and snow. Scandanavians, for example, would never see snow as an impediment – of society, or of things of the heart.

This is what makes Minnesotans strong. Possibly, it is also what makes Irish people impervious to the long, penetrating melancholy of rain.

PART THREE

Poets of the South

The Accents of the South

I walk this literary city in the exhausted calm of late December. It is 8.35 a.m. on the last day of 1996. The streets are bleak and subdued. People at St Lukes who are waiting for the Number 8 bus into town look like the Friday evening stragglers in a dentist's waiting room. Exhausted, but resigned to the pain. I decide to skip the bus and keep walking, down Summerhill North, along McCurtain Street, passing Isaac's Restaurant window, down into Bridge Street where I still expect to see the Mercier Bookshop, but it has now fled across the Lee to French Church Street. It was in the Mercier Bookshop that my first collection of poems was launched, a mighty shindig organised by Sean Bohan, the ebullient City Librarian. I will never forget Claud Cockburn, ill but holding forth to a group of adoring postgraduate history students, with Patricia, his wife, telling him to steady on. That's nearly twenty years ago. Twenty years is just about enough time to scratch at the literary surface of Cork, a buttery marsh of a metropolis that hoards and preserves whole centuries of published poets and novelists.

On my way to the City Library I pass through Paul Street, once the bleak warehouse district, but now a book-lover's paradise, with Connolly's, Collins, Mercier and Waterstones. Bookshops, like shoe-stores, always seem to thrive in clusters. In this, bookshops are just like poets. Booksellers are gregarious creatures. It is the nature of the business. Once upon a time there was a cluster of bookshops at the end of Oliver Plunkett Street, the APCK, Liam Ruiseal's (still there), Tom Trahy's, but now the centre of gravity has shifted to what Con Collins, publisher and bookseller, always refers to as the

Huguenot Quarter. With Waterstones as a kind of heavy anchor, the bookstores are unlikely to slip their present moorings for a long time. It's interesting that the current crop of bookshops have returned to the original district of the famous Bolster's of the early nineteenth century. At the end of our millenium the book-trade, at least, has come full circle.

'It is the taste for literature, stimulated and nourished by the Cork Library and the Cork Institution, the diocesan and many private libraries, that has given the city such literary repute, and enabled her to produce a host of crack writers,' wrote Brian A Cody in 1859. Cody's host of writers would have included Callanan, Father Prout and Windele. Callanan was an interesting creature, an educated Loyal Catholic who died too young to be politicised by the *Young Irelanders* or that famous Mallowman, Thomas Davis. Born in 1795, Callanan was educated at Sullivan's School in Cork City and Dr Harrington's in Cobh from where he entered Maynooth to study for the priesthood. Like many who followed, it was his parents rather than himself who had the vocation. He left Maynooth in the summer of 1815, but went back again just to placate his father. His second attempt didn't last long. By 1816 he was attending Trinity College, this time studying medicine.

At Trinity – inspired by Byron and two TCD prizes in poetry – he began to take the vocation of poet very seriously. He left Trinity after two years, full of plans; for volumes of poems, a collection of songs, a very Yeatsean plan for a book of folktales. He moved idly between his sister's house and West Cork, like any young artist of today waiting for an Arts Council grant:

The Recluse of Inchidony

Once more I'm free – the city's din is gone,
and with it wasted days and weary nights;

But bitter thoughts will sometimes rush upon
The heart that ever lov'd its sounds or sights ...

Bard of my boyhood's love, farewell to thee!
I little deem'd that e'er my feeble lay
Should wait thy doom – those eyes so soon should see
The clouding of thy spirits glorious ray;
Fountain of beauty, on life's desert way
Too soon thy voice is hush'd, thy waters dried:
Eagle of song, too short thy pinion's sway
Career'd in its high element of pride,
Weep, blue-eyed Albyn, weep! With him thy glory died!'

'The Recluse' is a complex poem, one of the best ever written by a Corkman. The language is too decorative for our modern taste, but if we were to set aside our modern contextual ignorance and impatience as well as our indifference to non-political material, we would discover an entirely new kind of Corkman, a romantic patriot with a deep faith in the civilising project of the British Empire. Only a citizen of Cork well educated, socially confident, versed in Greek history and antiquity, could have walked the wind-swept beach of Inchidony and thrived on Romantic Loyalism like this:

England, thou freest, noblest of the world!
O may the minstrel never live to see
Against thy sons the flag of green unfurl'd,

Or his own land thus aim at liberty;
May their sole rivalry for ever be
Such as the Gallic despot dearly knew,
When English hearts and Irish chivalry
Strove who should first be where the eagle flew,
And high their conquering shout arose o'er Waterloo.

The poem is essentially a lament on the death of Byron, but also a lament for Callanan's own misspent education. A poem of excuses, like every Romantic poem, but brilliant in its personal voice: *The load of life that did my spirit bow/ Was hid beneath a calm or mirthful mein.*

After a short burst of teaching at Mr Lynch's Everton School in Cork, Callanan left Ireland for Lisbon. In Portugal he was thrown in upon himself. His was a personal exile, brilliantly so. In a notebook he wrote: 'Christmas Eve, 1827. This night twelvemonth I was in Clonakilty with dear friends; this night I am alone in a land of strangers, but, as I purpose, Please God, I seek to be alone with God, I shall be happy anywhere.'

Callanan's presence is a strong and intriguing one in Munster literature. He sits on the saddle of two centuries and two sensibilities. Munster nationalists of the late nineteenth century must have found him very odd, or at least fragmented. Topography and topographical poems are the great saviours of talents that are politically doubtful. I often think that Pasternak survived numerous purges because his poems were full of love for Moscow as well as Georgia. Love of the native place allowed many Anglo-Irish writers, for example, to be appropriated into the Nation's project. Callanan was not Anglo-Irish in any sense of the word. He wrote his long poem 'Accession Of George The Fourth' (*And joyous thousands loudly shout,/ Huzza for George Our King!*) because he was an Irishman who was a British subject. Parts of that British past inspired him. In many of his poems his love of Greece shines through. Greek freedom was one of his abiding passions. Much of his enthusiasm for Greece must have come from Byron, but Callanan worked his own magic with Hellenic subjects. In 'The Restoration of the Spoils of Athens', one of his Trinity Prize poems, he writes:

Ere one Athenian should remain
To languish life in captive chain,
Or basely wield a freeman's sword
Beneath a Macedonian lord!
Such, then, was Greece, tho' conquer'd, chained,
Some pride, some virtue, yet remained …

As with Greece, so it was with Irish subject matter. Callanan didn't shun it. But Irish history was just one more curiosity to be investigated and remade in art. In 'The Revenge of Donal Comm' and 'Dirge of O'Sullivan Bear' he recasts stories of two great chieftains of West Cork. The 'Dirge' is a fine piece of tight invective and spell-binding. In these poems, Callanan indulges his Gothic and Ossianic streaks:

A curse, blessed ocean,
Is on thy green water,
From the haven of Cork
To Ivera of slaughter,
Since the billows were dyed
With the red wound of fear,
Of Muiertach Oge,
Our O'Sullivan Bear

('Dirge of O Sullivan Bear')

Much of his historical poems are in that vein, as are many of the translations from the Irish. In his note 'Translations from the Irish' he writes like a proper Regency gentleman:

Though the Irish are undoubtedly of a poetic temperament, yet the popular songs of the lower order are neither numerous, nor in general possessed of much beauty … The Poets of the populace confined themselves chiefly to Irish – a tongue which, whatever may be its capabilities, had ceased to be the language of the great and polished for centuries before the poetic taste revived in Europe. They were compelled to use a despised dialect, which, moreover, the political divisions of the country had rendered an object of suspicion to the ruling powers. The Government and the populace were indeed so decidedly at variance, that the topics which the village Bards were obliged to select were such as often to render the indulgence of their poetic powers rather dangerous. Their heroes were frequently inmates of jails or doomed to the gibbet, and the severe criticism of the cat-o'-nine tails might be the lot of the panygerist ... The following songs are specimens of the popular poetry of later days. I have translated them as closely as possible, and present them to the public more as literary curiosities than on any other account.

And so it was. Callanan dismissed the literary reputation of anything in Irish from the Jacobite Wars onward. We can't blame him too much that he missed O'Bruadair, Merriman, Eibhlin Ní Chonaill as well as much of the folksong. After all, Corkery's *Hidden Ireland* hadn't appeared. To an educated Corkman in 1816 that Gaelic aspect of Ireland was not so much invisible as awaiting improvement through English.

Callanan never returned to Cork. He died abroad like his hero, Byron. His work does repay careful reading and study. Someday perhaps a young scholar at UCC or elsewhere will put his life in context with a full biography. The same scholar might achieve what I failed to achieve a few years ago – to find his burial-place in Lisbon. Though his spiritual burial-place is well marked, for all to see and read:

> *There is a green island in lone Gougane Barra,*
> *Where Allua of songs rushes forth as an arrow;*
> *In deep-valley'd Desmond – a thousand wild fountains*
> *Come down to that lake, from their home in the*
> *mountains.*

There grows the wild ash, and a time-stricken willow
Looks chidingly down on the mirth of the billow ...

('Gougane Barra')

Another Cork literary genius was Francis Sylvester Mahony, who used the pen-name Father Prout, a Jesuit-educated, pre-Joycian Joyce. Mahoney's elaborate, witty, classical prose fell foul of the Celtic Twilight and the cultural seriousness of the national movement. Mahoney was an anthologist of styles and languages, an intellectual snob who was so out of it politically that he hated Daniel O'Connell. Mahony-Prout was born in Cork on 31 December, 1804. The Jesuits educated him from the age of eleven, at Clongowes, Paris, St Acheul, Rome and Freiberg. Released by the frustrated and exhausted Jesuit Order, he was ordained a priest in Lucca, by what Rev George O'Neill, SJ called 'a kindly but imprudent prelate'.

After ordination he returned to Cork where – without the local Bishop's authority – he decided to build a 'chapel-at ease' to the North Cathedral. After the poor Bishop had the temerity to put a stop to Prout's plans, the priest-genius headed for London and more welcoming pastures. In London he met two other brilliant Corkmen, Maginn, the editor of *Fraser's Magazine*, and Daniel Maclise, the genial painter and illustrator. It's interesting that Maclise and Maginn had changed the spelling of their surnames, from McLise and McGinn; surely a sign of the socialisation process going in polite Irish society around the time of the Union. Mahony's first contribution to *Fraser's* was 'Father Prout's Apology for Lent'. Part of the joke of his pen-name was that there really was a Father Prout, a dull and simple Parish Priest of Watergrasshill who had often visited Mahony's father in Cork. In the manner of Flann O'Brien, Mahony invented an editor for Prout who offered comments on Prout's writings. The *Fraser's* contributions were published as *The Reliques of Father Prout* in 1859. One of the best essays 'The Roqueries of Tom Moore' is supposed to be a catalogue of Moore's plagiarisms:

Among the Romans, whoever stole a child was liable by law to get a soundflogging; and as *plaga* in Latin means a *stripe* or *lash*, kidnappers in Cicero's time were called *plagiarii* or cat-o'-nine-tail-villians. I approve highly of this law of the twelve tables; but perhaps my judgement is biased and I should be an unfair juror to give a verdict in a case which comes home to my own feelings so poignantly. The term *plagiary* has since been applied metaphorically to literary shop-lifters and book-robbers, who stuff their pages with other men's goods and thrive on indiscriminate pillage. This is justly considered a high misdemeanour in the republic of letters, and the lash of criticism is unsparingly dealt on pickpockets of this description. Among the Latins, Martial is the only classic author by whom the term *plagiarius* is used in the metaphorical sense as applied to literature .... Cicero himself was accused by the Greeks of pilfering whole passages .... Virgil being accused of taking whole similes from Homer, gloried in the theft .... It is well known that Menander and Aristophanes were mercilessly pillaged by Terence and Plautus .... The Blarney Stone in my neighbourhood has attracted hither many an illustrious visitor; but none has been so assiduous in my time as Tom Moore. While he was engaged in his best and most unexceptional work on the melodious ballads of his country, he came regularly every summer, and did me the honour to share my humble roof repeatedly. He knows well how often he plagued me to supply him with original songs I had picked up in France among merry troubadours and carol-loving inhabitants of that once happy land, and to what extent he has transferred these foreign inventions into the 'Irish Melodies' .... It would be easy to point out detached fragments and stray metaphors, which he has scattered here and there in such gay confusion that every page has within its limits a mass of felony and plagiarism sufficient to hang him.

Prout goes on to accuse Moore of stealing his 'The Shandon Bells', written in Rome, in order to produce the inferior 'Evening Bells, a Petersburg Air'. It is a tribute to Mahony's swift obscurity that serious anthologists never remember that 'The Bells of Shandon' was written as part of an elaborate literary joke. Plagiarism, with its roots in kidnapping, was supposedly important to Prout because he claimed to have been kidnapped by the inventor of Wood's Halfpence who was jealous of this child (the urchin Prout) because he was the natural son of Dean Swift and Stella. In Mahony's prose nothing was ever simple.

Another marvellous essay of Prout's is 'Literature and the Jesuits', one of the most compelling eulogies ever written. In style, poetry and sanguinity, it rivals Edmund Burke. I can imagine the young Joyce at Clongowes reading this hymn to Jesuit excellence. As far as Prout was concerned there were only two Orders in the Catholic Church, the Jesuits and the Dominicans. All the others were no better than barbarians:

> The Jesuits, in every University to which they could get access, broke new ground. Indefatigable in their pursuit, the new professors made incessant inroads into the domains of ignorance and sloth .... D'Olivet, Fontenelle, Crebillon, Le Franc de Pompignan – there is scarcely a name known to literature during the seventeenth century which does not bear witness to their prowess in the province of education.

And this great eulogy came from someone writing for a very anti-Romish audience, someone confident enough of his style and his facts. It is interesting to note that Mahony's best work was concentrated into his *Fraser's* years, between 1834 and 1837. After 1837 Prout's genius was transferred to *Bentley's Magazine*, then edited by Charles Dickens. Twenty years later, Prout's name did still count for something. He was sought out by Thackery for an Ode to mark the founding of the *Cornhill Magazine*.

In 1846 Mahony became the Rome Correspondent for the London *Daily News*. Twelve years later he moved to Paris to become Correspondent for *The Globe*. He died in Paris on 18 May, 1866, still implacable in his hatred of Daniel O'Connell, still refusing to contribute to *The Nation*, yet reciting the daily office of a Catholic priest to the end. In his centenary lecture to a more nationally minded crowd in 1905, Father O'Neill noted 'We have to regret that Mahony never did anything for Irish journalism.... Among the myrtles and passion-flowers of the Young Ireland poetry and rhetoric, Prout's glitter of epigram and gaiety would have been a pleasant and valuable variety.'

But Cork's first modern contribution to literature begins with the novels of Canon Sheehan and the elegant political prose essays of Justin McCarthy, MP. The swan-infested poems of Spenser, the Augustan wit of Berkeley and the county novels of Elizabeth Bowen could also be considered a part of the more pluralist local tradition.

But it wasn't until Daniel Corkery published his *Threshold of Quiet* in 1917 that the genuine petit-bourgeois atmosphere of the city came to light. Nowadays one associates Corkery's name with a narrow form of rural nationalism. But in 1907 Corkery wrote in his diary, 'I do not remember a schoolteacher being introduced into any modern novel – the modern novel does not deal with the middle-class'. Ten years later he published his Cork novel, a book full of melancholy cries and descriptions of escape – one character's escape into books, another's escape to the sea, yet another's escape through suicide.

The atmosphere of melancholy and stultifying piety had a profound effect on Corkery's more gifted successors, O'Faolain and O'Connor. Their Cork heroes also felt a desire to escape from the custody of their native place. O'Faolain's *Bird Alone* and O'Connor's *Dutch Interior* are crippled by excessive pieties. There are too many parents, too many virgins, too many hesitations. Forty years after the publication of *The Threshold of Quiet*, Corkery's influence on local writers was still very potent. Yet we tend to forget that O'Connor and O'Faolain were artists, not sociologists. Within their work is evidence of the life that was lived in provincial Ireland, but, even more so, evidence of their infinite capacity to take pains over their art.

David Marcus published his *To Next Year in Jerusalem* in 1954. It is the story of a Jewish family and a Jewish hero, Jonathan, who must choose between his Jewish orthodoxy, and his chairmanship of a Catholic club and Aileen his Christian beloved. Again, there is a restrictive familial atmosphere that owes as much to the Hail Mary as to the Havdullach.

Because novels and autobiographies are more influential than poems, outsiders have taken their image of literary Cork from the prose writers. For this reason alone the public perception of local life is nearly three decades out of date. It fascinates me that the dominant Cork books are O'Connor's *An Only Child* and O'Faolain's *Vive Moi*. Autobiographies appear in Cork City with the regularity of butter from Ballyclough or chickens from Cappoquin. Cork's sense of itself is heavily dependent upon the assembly of memory. Memory rather than art is the major contrivance that writers depend upon. I am guilty of it myself. But it is interesting to note that *An Only Child, To School Through the Fields, Song for a Poor Boy* and *Maura's Boy* are names more powerful than any Cork play or novel of the last two decades. What do these books mean? Do they spring from a powerful sense that everything personal might be lost; that such a loss might be greater than the loss of a novel or a play? They do tell us, more urgently than art, that Cork life is viable, and *significant* because it can be remembered so completely.

Between the prime of the great O'Connor and O'Faolain and today one must insert the liberal Sixties, the Beatles' many

LPs and the influence of healthy sex lives. Even in the 1950s, that decade of darkness and retrenchment, David Marcus had begun his *Poetry Ireland,* that later became *Irish Writing.* It was from Adelaide Street in Cork that Marcus published Denis Devlin's 'Heavenly Foreigner'. Seán Ó Ríordáin had launched his career at that time with *Eireaball Spideóige,* a collection that was ablaze with mid-century anxiety, humanity and cosmopolitan curiosity.

By the 1960s a group of poets – Seán O'Criadáin, Sean Lucy, Robert O'Donoghue, Patrick Galvin, Anthony Blinco – had emerged to blow away the petit-bourgeois pieties with surreal techniques and a deliberately internationalist outlook. Lucy explored Eliot, Galvin discovered Lorca and published 'Christ in London'. O'Criadáin ended up writing, with the encouragement of Princess Caetani of *Botteghe Oscure.*

'Nothwithstanding the unquestionable love of letters, strange to say, periodical literature never succeeded in Cork,' Cody again wrote in 1859. The number of short-lived literary magazines begun in Cork includes *The Monthly Miscellany* (1775), *The Hesperian Magazine* (1794) and *The Cork Magazine* (1847). In recent years *The Cork Review,* published by the Triskel Arts Centre, was edited by Paul Durcan and Tina Neylon. It was the best attempt ever made to produce a broadly-based arts magazine. The failure of Cork's literary magazines has nothing to do with the intellectual inferiority of a local literati: it has everything to do with the reluctance of moneyed institutions to sacrifice money for the sake of a good idea. In the last ten years especially, a rather nasty level of accountancy has crept into the sponsorship of arts projects. One can only live in hope that the obsession with numbers won't destroy funding entirely. Brave people like Paul Durcan, Tina Neylon or Seán Dunne never worried about the number of votes, or moral brownie-points, they might accumulate when they edited those excellent issues of *The Cork Review.* In the world of the arts we must encourage people to be brave – to do what is right and creative even if this is visible to small numbers only. The Cork periodicals that have survived, like *The Quarryman* and *The Holly Bough* are attached to moneyed ventures like the university and the Examiner Group.

Mention of Paul Durcan reminds me yet again of how positive and creative was that poet's sojourn in Cork:

> *We lived in a remote dower house in Cork*
> *Leaving the doors and windows always unlocked.*

('The Berlin Wall Café')

Durcan used to write an excellent column in *The Examiner*, a weekly feature to which many readers looked forward. Far from being eccentric or capricious, a kind of character that people like to paint for him in his absence, Durcan was incredibly generous and encouraging towards very young poets. His instincts were astonishingly well-grounded, and he can still read character better than anyone I know. Durcan absorbed the social atmosphere of Cork very well, and he is the only person I know who understands all the nuances of the Cork middle-class accent; pompous nasal Montenette, dim-witted Blackrock, daft-confused County and deadly-sharp Coal Quay. He has an actor's ear. A terrific mimic, his public reading of poems from *Sam's Cross* and *Teresa's Bar* have an edge and a wisdom that is positively eighteenth-century in its sharpness:

> *Such is the loyalty of his flock*
> *That on hearing that their bishop had murdered his wife*
> *Their immediate response was not of sympathy for the*
> * deceased*
> *But of regret that their bishop had ever got married:*
> *Said one old-timer by the Lough*

'He is a decent man – he should have stayed single.'
And an old virago in a hood-cloak in the Glen
   descanted
'Oh the wicked trollop – oh the poor old boyo.'

('Sam's Cross')

One writer, slightly younger than Durcan, who has gone on to produce a whole bookshelf of critical and creative work is Robert Welch. Like the poet O'Tuama, Welch's creative work has been hidden behind an influential academic and critical career. It is ironic (the irony of it never ceases to amaze me) that commentary can be more influential than created work. Yet, in his collection *Muskerry* (1991) Welch has produced a fine sequence of lyrics 'A House of the Kearneys'. This work, very much in the same mode as O'Tuama's 'Maymount: *Tigh Victeoireach a Leagadh*', is a poem of family, memory, and sharp analysis:

In suffering everything becomes secret; even
the smallest venture, buying a frock
or pair of shoes, is fraught with danger.
The heart's all hunger.

Suspicion is everywhere. You saw
Your father low over the cranked handle
Of a Crossley Tender; his thin body so frail
How could he not go blind?

Everything burned with malevolence in the corner shop:
The smell of bread, the rich savour of smoked ham,
The array of cakes in the wooden tray, all
Charged with hate.

A sense of history, a complex and contradictory retelling of the material, is part of Welch's gift as a poet and novelist. He has written a novel in Irish as well as a Spenserian novella, *The Kilcolman Notebook*. Recently Robert Welch has produced his most ambitious creative work, a novel, *Groundwork,* that weaves history, sociology, sex and class into an inclusive, political, love story:

1903
Mary O'Dwyer

I decided to go up onto the deck when the word went round that we were coming up to Dunkettle Bridge. I leaned against the railings and looked towards Glanmire, and at the dark stretch of water beyond the bridge. The tide was out, so the sloblands alongside the river were visible in the soft grey sameness. The rain slanted down. I could feel the coldness of the rail pressing against my slightly swollen stomach. I was now three months gone and hardly showing.

I couldn't stick it any longer with Jim in Leeds, so I came back to have the baby, disgrace or no disgrace ...

The novel is a personal story, or several stories, with an interleaved structure that is more truthful about Irish society than any other novel where there is a pretence of social cohesion. It is the high-point of Walch's artistic life to date.

Since Gregory O'Donoghue published *Kicking* in 1975 and Michael Davitt edited *Innti,* a new generation of writers has emerged in Cork. The young poets have developed a supportive community. Gone are the bourgeois pieties and the sidelong glances. O'Donoghue's poetry is cool and controlled, as in 'Youghal Abbey':

> *Green stone a few trees lean to, perfect sheol, though I do*
> *Not imagine the dead have truck with this; unless,*

Leaking their toenails into bark & bole and
dead are green itself.
In which case they are the colour of space the eye
depends on.

Born in 1951, educated at UCC and at Kingston, Ontario, O'Donoghue has lived a life of reticence and silence, very much like the calm, methodical seriousness of the nineteenth-century Callanan. His 1995 pamphlet from Three Spires Press, *The Permanent Way*, was a sequence of lyrics that used to brilliant effect the vocabulary and weighty metaphors from his time as an employee of British Rail. In 'Goods Train' he details a creative coming-together in the manner of Frost:

Only when you've cleared the sidings and curve
off the feeding road onto the fast road,
when the clatters over the points gives way

to rhythm, can you know it all might hold together.
Just about – like today's gallivanting wagons,
Frisky, yet not over-light on their flanges . . . .

Another poet with O'Donoghue's delicate touch is Maurice Riordan, whose first collection *A Word from the Loki* was published by Faber in 1995. Riordan was also a tutor in the UCC English Department in the mid-Seventies. He has a great delicacy of touch, the rhythm of the Dolmen Mandarin style, but combines this talent with an urbane, knowing, cocky humour. His poem 'Fish' is a good example of this:

. . . Think of the silky salmon mousse,
the peppery clout of my bisque Normandie!
Latterly my tastes veered oriental: saffron,
Lemon grass, the cool transparencies of Japan . . .

But now what can I do: when, after ten years,
You announce that, truly, you detest fish.

The fact that he has other poems, 'Steak', 'Apples', 'Milk'
and 'The Table', all turning on urbane sketches of post-Modern
domestic banalities, should be sufficient warning to all and
sundry in Cork that a really new talent, a Louis MacNeice of
the South, has arrived at last:

The Table

It would require work. That marbled green veneer
would have to go, along with several nicks
and gouges, obscure stains, other people's memories.

Another poet of the O'Donoghue clan (which clan seems
particularly gifted in recent years – think of Emma Donoghue,
the novelist, and that superbly talented Oxford-based poet,
Bernard O'Donoghue, whose *Gunpowder* (Chatto) exploded
triumphantly across the literary scene last year) another poet of
the O'Donoghue's is Liz O'Donoghue, a very sparky, cocky
and individualistic poet. She has organised the Live Poets
Readings for many years in various cafes and pubs, but
especially in the High-B Bar in Cork. She is a great love poet.
'Living with you\is ruining my eyesight' she tells one lover who
keeps sending photographs. Yet another love-poem, 'Poem on
Emigration', operates at two or three levels, its speaker full of
bitterness and caution:

I should compare you
to Cronus, the father of Zeus
who swallowed his children at birth
so that they would not overthrow him
and I should give you a stone and a bitter pill

to disgorge
all those you've swallowed.

Liz O'Donoghue is certainly one of the new talents upon whom a great deal of hope is fixed. Another poet born in the Sixties is Patrick Cotter, a sharp and gifted poet whose reading of Rilke and poets of Eastern Europe has given him a sense of history and a vocabulary that is entirely new. Cotter is a fine love-poet, yet he is the least romantic in terms of tone and language, and he uses the language of the senses even in his poetry of politics:

> *Parched earth of daybreak we eat you at sundown*
> *we eat you at noon in the morning we eat you at night*
> *we eat you and eat you*
> *a man lives in a whitehouse he slithers with the rattlers*
> *he types*
> *he types when dusk falls on California ...*

Then there are the Irish language poets of this city, the ones who might have been rejected by Father Prout or J J Callanan, or who might have faced the cat-o'-nine-tails of the City Sheriff for praise of Raparees or 'Tory' friends. For years Cork was an English city, indeed the mere Irish had to get special permission to remain within the city limits after sundown. It is an ancient ordinance that could be invoked usefully even today. But even in the eighteenth century Irish was spoken in Cork, manuscripts were collected and protected by people like Bishop Murphy who wanted to be able to speak Irish to the country people at Confirmation time. However, it would be fair to say that there's more Irish spoken now in Cork City than at any time in history. The gifted Irish language poets of our day, Sean Ó Tuama, Liam Ó Muirthile, Micheal Davitt and Louis de Paor, didn't just appear out of thin air. The air of Cork that they inhaled already had Irish in it.

Thomas McCarthy

It is impossible to walk the streets of Cork without thinking of Seán Ó Ríordáin, the greatest of them all. He was a Clerical Officer in the motor-tax office, a genius among the 'Halla' men. I still meet people who worked in City Hall who can recount hilarious – even scary stories – about Ó Ríordáin. Each day when I wait at the pedestrian lights at the infernally busy corner of Grand Parade and Washington Street, I think of Ó Ríordáin's masterful poem *'Suile Donna'*. Seán Ó Coileain in his biographical study of the poet published by Clochomhar in 1982 reproduces that part of the Diary which contains the genesis of the poem:

> Tráthnóna inné bhuaileas le buachaill scoile, sé no seacht mblíana déag. Cuireadh in aithne dhom é. Duradh liom cé hí a mháthair. Tá aithne agam uirthi. Lil Ní Shuilleabháin ab ainm dí tráth. Ansan thugas a suile súid fé ndeara ina cheann so. Thitfeadh aon fear i ngrá lei mar mhaithe lena súile amháin.

He saw the son of a woman whose eyes had captivated him; out of which he made one of the most exquisite lyrics written in Irish or English:

> *Is léi na súile donna so*
> *chím i bplaosc a mic,*
> *Ba theangmháil le háilleact é,*
> *A suile a thuirlingt ort;*
>
> *Ba theangmháil phribhléideach é,*
> *Lena meabhair is lena corp,*
> *Is míle bliain ba ghearr leat é,*
> *Is iad ag féachaint ort.*
>
> ('Línte Liombó')

That poem is often in my head, haunting the atmosphere of the evening, as I wait for the pedestrian lights to go green.

Ó Ríordáin's presence is very strong for me, part of the atmosphere of the city centre, as well as a haunting echo whenever I walk on College Road or Donovan's Road.

But the new Irish poets have created their own atmosphere and their own time-space. Sean Ó Tuama, for example, who was one of the first champions of Ó Ríordáin's poetry, has literally taken flight from the damp material of consumptive cottages. His best collection of poems by far is *An Bás I dTír na nÓg*. His Land of Youth is Greece, especially Crete. In this sun-drenched, body-affirming land, Ó Tuama has made a new kind of poetry and prose-poetry:

> *Anois an t-am don rince aonair*
> *ar ghainimh bheo na trá –*
> *na cosa a chaitheamh go h aiféiseach*
> *is lea d'aonghnó sa teas.*

('An Bás i dTír na nÓg')

Ó Tuama is a heat-seeker, a life-giver, a lover of everything sensuous, as one could only expect from the author of *Grá in Amhráin na nDaoine* (1960).

Liam Ó Muirthile, a younger poet, continues Ó Ríordáin's serious journalism – the task of writing an *Irish Times* column. But the theme and tone of Ó Muirthile's work is still very much his own:

Jazz Musician

> *Níl sa gealach amuigh*
> *anocht ach spotsholas eile*
> *A aimsíonn tine dhraíochta*
> *Ina fheadóg mhór;*
> *Scinneann lasracha*
> *Óna ghá airgid.*

Michael Davitt, the leading light of his generation, now lives in Dublin where he is a producer with RTÉ. His most famous poem is undoubtedly 'An Scathán', 'The Mirror', in which he deals with the painful theme of fathers. It is a much anthologised work:

> *Ag maisiú a tseamra chodlata do*
> *d'ardaigh se an scathán anuas*
> *gan lamh chúnta a iarradh;*
> *ar ball d'iompaigh dath na cré air,*
> *an oiche sin phleasc a chroí.*

> *Decorating the bedroom himself*
> *he hoisted the great mirror*
> *without asking for any help; then the colour of earth*
> *came on him,*
> *that night his heart gave in.*

But there are other poems equally stunning, spread across three fine collections, published in 1982, 1983 and 1993. His *Selected Poems*, a bilingual edition, was published in 1987 and should be owned by anyone interested in Cork poetry after Ó Ríordáin.

Louis de Paor is another superb Irish language poet, born in the Sixties and full of the intensity and sense of purpose of writers who were educated in UCC by Seán Ó Tuama. Not that he is po-faced or without humour. He wears his Doctorate very lightly indeed, and in a poem like 'Gaeilgeoiri' his rascally nature is evident:

> *Ó cé, níor chuireamar Pinnochio,*
> *ár dTaoiseach caincíneach as oifig.*

> *Níor bhain an saighdiúir*
> *a mhéar thais den truicear aclaí*

chun toitín a dhearadh don sceimhlitheoir
sceimhlithe.

Níor tháinig an Dr. Paisley ná Easpag Luimní
go dtí na ranganna éacúiméineacha
i gClub an Chonartha.

('30 Dán')

The richness of the Cork scene is everywhere. It's true that Cork has suffered greatly in terms of perception abroad ('abroad' being anywhere farther north than Mitchelstown), so that outsiders haven't grasped the energy at work in the South. In the future I can see a much greater appreciation of Cork writers, a true estimation of the achievement of Daniel Corkery and the narrative social realism of his best urban stories and his novel. O'Connor and O'Faolain will always remain bench-mark story-writers, if not as good as the Russians, at least as serious in their dedication to the craft of the story. With the development of the Munster Literature Centre, the nurturing of the workshops of The Cork Womens' Poetry Circle and the expansion of the Triskel Arts Centre as venue and meeting-place, a young Cork writer need never have to shelter in a doorway from the rain.

The new poets have been inspired, outraged, stimulated and encouraged by the two main movements in contemporary Irish poetry – the Ulster Poets and the Women's Movement. For over two decades Ulster writing has been ever present in Cork in the person of John Montague. In the Seventies his home in Grattan Hill on the eastern fringe of Cork City was a welcoming place for student poets like Theo Dorgan, Patrick Crotty and Maurice Riordan. It was in that house between 1974 and 1978 that John and Evelyn hosted a series of terrific parties where new poets met with writers like Seamus Heaney, Derek Mahon, Michael Longley, as well as Hugh MacDiarmid and

Thomas McCarthy

Robert Graves. Looking back now I can see that Montague's house was a kind of market-place, rather like Daniel Corkery's house, where poets, composers and artists met.

It is true that communities of Irish writers tend to be male-dominated, conservative and encouraging of that age-old Irish tendancy to make connections and negotiate power in a 'laddish' manner. In the mid-Seventies there were few role-models for a female poet to follow. Ironically, the women writers were there – B G MacCarthy, Elizabeth Bowen and Eiléan Ní Chuilleanáin. But young writers don't come to their talent with a complete bibliography. They need to be educated, led, pointed in the direction of some magnificent bookshelves. In 1975 in Cork where could a woman poet go to be inspired and affirmed? The women writers who emerged, novelist Mary Leland, dramatist and editor Maeve Saunders, poet Liz O'Donoghue, are writers who came through on their own. Each in her own way is a loner, a Dervla Murphy rather than a Jenny Wyse-Power.

In the mid-Eighties Maire Bradshaw set up the Cork Women's Poetry Circle. For the last ten years this has been one of the most important forums for discussions, seminars, workshops and readings. Bradshaw has been a major facilitator of women's writing. In recent years she has introduced really enthusiastic and truly underfunded groups of women to poets like Eavan Boland and Máire Mhac an tSaoí. At the other side of town, passionately community-based and politically intelligent, Mary Johnson has developed the Munster Literature Centre on Sullivan's Quay. Here is one of those direct-action, anti-poverty programs that has blossomed into the major local authority on everything literary. The MLC with its readings, workshops and newsletter is now the main-mover in Cork's literary life. Johnson is one of those activists who can get everyone going in one direction at the same time. With poet Paddy Galvin she has organised cross-Channel reading circuits with Welsh writers and plans North-South exchanges. What is interesting is that these two women got things going in a directly political, community-based way. In a sense they wouldn't hang around waiting to be invited to someone's party. They created the party.

No young writer should now feel the need to escape from Cork in order to be a writer. The failure to produce the goods is not a failure of their native city but a failure of the imagination. The melancholia of six decades of prose has passed away. In its wake have come the flashing divers and screeching gulls of young poetry. As Ó Ríordáin noted in his Diary, *'Tá na tithe agus an áit go léir lán de smaointe chomh maith le duilleóga agus iad ag fás.'*

Golden Notebook of Dorgan's World

Of all the poets who inhabited the tree-muffled, hilltop campus of UCC in the mid-Seventies, Theo Dorgan was clearly the most poetic. I was too young by a year or two to have witnessed Nuala Ní Dhomhnaill's wildly red-haired and radical rites of passage, so that Theo D had very little competition in my circle in terms of personal style and romantic associations. In the student literary world he had a strong, combative presence that combined, with great ease, a well-read Marxist analysis of the place of culture in the 'revolution' and a deeply felt belief in the individualistic, holy nature of the poet. He could quote with equal venom and conviction from Marcuse's *One Dimensional Man* and from Robert Graves's *The White Goddess*. He believed in both the wily political skills of Gorky and the irresponsible lunacy of Baudelaire.

Theo had a gifted, mimetic intelligence so that he seemed fluent in everything, in revolution, high finance, the Stickies, Fianna Fáil, Kerry Irish and Left Bank French. Like many people who acquire vast quantities of knowledge without any seeming effort, Theo found it difficult to be taken seriously. As the late John Jordan before him discovered, a high IQ can be a positive disadvantage in provincial Irish life. Munster's self-contained bourgeois sons and daughters heading towards their Degrees found him just too anarchist and provocative. For myself, and a few others who were keeping our poetry low-key, Theo was a kind of one man Popular Front. He would be the successor to Paddy Galvin, we hoped, who wouldn't go into exile. And he might go on to organise things and deepen his soul in the process. This was a unique kind of destiny that I imagined for him. He didn't disappoint me.

We became close friends out of a shared dream of setting up a college literary magazine. The literary magazine is always the first dream place of a group of young poets. Around the same time William Wall, then writing under the name Liam de Bhal, had teamed up with John McCarg the printer to produce a beautiful magazine called *First Issue*. UCC already had a literary magazine, *The Quarryman*, that was published occasionally by an energetic and provocative Students' Union, but Theo and I hoped for something that would be entirely at the service of poets.

In our undergraduate years the people who are closest to us are those who share our dreams. In the years 1974 to 1979, the years of opening out to life and preparation for leave-taking, Theo and I became great friends. I visited him at his home in Redemption Road and met his father, a lovely gentle man who still lived in shock after the death of his young wife. I recognised in his family some of the survivor-heroism of educated, bookish working-class life that was typical of Sixties and Seventies urban Ireland. I could see in his father the same stoicism and sense of humour that was in my own family in Cappoquin – so different from the cliché-ridden vulgarity of poor Irish life that one sees on screen and in theatres. It's not the arrogance and ambition of the poor that literature betrays, it's their gentility. Talking to Theo's father and brothers, I was reminded yet again that literature fails the working class by its very nature. Literature communicates and makes connections like a borough politician. Being poor is not a social experience, it is private and unique to each family. It is something that each poor family has no wish to communicate, while retaining the right that their past struggles be honoured.

Not that Theo Dorgan was living at home. No way. At this stage he was carrying on a campaign to have all his Cork friends leave their family homes and set up in flats. His practical contribution to this campaign was that he appeared to move in with most of his friends temporarily. In the space of five or six years he had tried most neighbourhoods in Cork and most architectural environments, from a delapidated flat opposite Collins Barracks, a leaking tenement across the Victoria Hospital to a stylish detached residence on Lover's Walk complete with gardener. He was a completely modern man. Even then I had the measure of my own character, which was extremely sluggish and inert. But I observed his life with admiration and admired his dynamism as well as his personal style. Theo thought that there was too much attachment to apron-strings in our various circles in Cork. In this he was dead right. I'm not sure whether it was he or I invented the "old" Cork saying that "if you lose your virginity in Cork, someone will find it and bring it home to your mother". Together we started using it, telling it to every visiting writer to Cork who marvelled at old Cork's wisdom. Old writers are so gullible, we thought, they want to believe everything.

By 1977 most of the College poets who had spent their undergraduate years in the Kampus Kitchen had left UCC's hallowed hill. But Theo hung on until he completed his MA thesis on Robert Graves. Enduring College until the Masters Degree is completed is the first real sign of strong character. An abandoned thesis haunts one for life. I'd put away my old parka jacket and applied for jobs. Theo continued his work in the Arts world, seamlessly connecting his days as a student literary activist with a new career organising the literature programme of the new Triskel Arts Centre. Triskel was the further maturing, by the indefatigable Robbie MacDonald, of the combined arts idea begun in the old Tubular Gallery in Paul Street. Ten years later, after Triskel and the Cork Film Festival, Theo moved to Dublin to become Director of Poetry Ireland – a job and an organisation he has expanded and strengthened with characteristic *élan*.

I cannot read the poems of *Rosa Mundi*, his new collection, without feeling also the force of his great undergraduate personality, the past that has made him the kind of poet he is today. That he has survived as an artist is amazing. By this I mean that a lesser person would have lost the gift of verse under the stress and ambition of a career directing a very vulnerable and exposed arts organisation like Poetry Ireland. Our Republic is a land of anxious poets, weekend poets, summer poets, all operating with the expectation of public response and even acclamation. Each poet thinks of himself or herself as a key operator in a personal kingdom. I acknowledge the reality of a kingdom of my own, and defend its private borders. Dorgan the poet also feels that solitary exile of the poet's territory. In the poem 'Somewhere' he addresses the vital Rose of his world, his dead mother:

> *Mother, I have been in the cold places I dreamed of*
> *When you were proud of your bright son.*
> *The day the bus went by the back road to*
> *   Sheremetyevo*
> *I snatched beroizka from the rattle of pale trunks,*
> *The word echoing. Tracks of a rabbit in the snow,*
> *My own tracks crossing the trail of childhood.*

In *Rosa Mundi* there is a good deal of journeying, outward and away from the private centre of mere filial poetry. The private place is the waiting mother, the firelight, the soup, that place where trails seem to lead back to. Yet in the poem he repeats the line *'somewhere there is a simple life'* as if he knew that he can never get back to it. The refrain in a poem is always the flag of a lost hope. Reviewing the *Selected Poems* of Robert Graves in a recent *Poetry Ireland Review*, Dorgan wrote 'His poetic universe is a habitable ecology where the heart anchors us in a place tossed by wind and thought, stable under slow-revolving heavens. It is a place where the truth and life of myth is both urgent and evident'. Part of the force of *Rosa Mundi* is that placing of urgent truths in differing landscapes, from the winding country road of County Armagh, to a grain of sand in Syria:

> *Aeons watched mountains fold over into dust.*
> *Hedged armies manouvred and clashed,*
> *Stoop-bellied ships worked out the warp and weft*
> *until cartographers with their black arts*
> *Trammelled the globe to a version of itself.*

In Dorgan's work, the intelligence is always socialist while the feeling is holy and Gravesian. 'My blood and my brain are bound to his rule' he says in 'Mercury'. The poems in this book fall into those two general categories: love and travel, love and public life, love and history, love and the future. In his poem to the last Ambassador of the Soviet Union to Ireland, 'To Gennadi Uranov in the Coming Times', he combines both categories, brain and blood. His sense of the ending of an era in Russian history, a Russia he knows well from travelling there, is offered as a series of feelings rather than political insights. In this way it is more effective as a poem, closer to the gigantic shift in feeling that constitutes political change in a vast country. The image of *'starlight of prisons'* dovetails neatly into the Irish experience of Kilmainham Gaol: *'Before the lights go down we examine each other/ shyly.'*

And so the poems go on, following a definite pattern of feelings but turning on the fulcrum of the private poetic kingdom. (I use the word 'kingdom' deliberately, for in the Gravesian world the poet's life is not something achieved by a majority vote. On the contrary, it is a born elect.) One can see in Dorgan's work the working out of that tension – between the ideas of justice and the feelings of the holy. The one binding theme in Dorgan's work, that most Gravesian theme, is adult love. The setting for a great deal of his thought, political, familial, national, is the lovers' apartment. This is what gives such a feeling of youthfulness and contemporariness to even the most archaic expressions and formal mannerisms in his verse. In 'House over the Harbour at Ballintoy' he says:

> Not a room in that house where a man or
> woman could
> Stretch out, built by an artist to face down the
> nights
>
> ... The strange house
> Is a watchtower for times of shallow sleep, when
> boats at night
> Make the skin crawl like the sea.

It is the skin that crawls, not the boats that cover the sea. The world impinges upon *'the ordinary house of love'*, to use a description from Dorgan's previous collection. Whatever desperate things come by water and by night are filtered through the architecture and activity of adult love. The core of this new book, then, is the sequence of love poems. Although sequence may be too strong a word here: the love lyrics are not sequenced in a formal sense by numbers or italics. But they do have the power of a single coherence, rather like entries in the diary of a character in a novel – a kind of *Golden Notebook* of love as a main character. In a radical sense Dorgan has worked towards the kind of interpersonal salvation pursued by the young and the disorientated in Doris Lessing's fiction.

'*I hear dustmotes falling like leaves on the/ counterpane,*' he writes in 'A Slow Poem', trying to describe the absolute stillness of lovers in a room. In the next poem 'The Backward Look' (a title so full of resonances, from Frank O'Connor and John Osborne) he describes the high summer of early domesticity: '*Our kitchen. Our first/ summer. This life.*'

172

It is love that's the Rose of the World. The true Rosa Mundi. Robert Welch, a Cork poet and scholar of the Spenserian world, captures the essence of Dorgan's achievement in a recent *Poetry Ireland Review*:

> The sharp and plangent recognition of the force and energy in others and in life itself is not, I think, something that can be faked. Much else can, but this, which marks out the really serious artist, is either there or it's not; and it declares itself throughout these poems at the centre of the book.

What happens in this new collection is that the mother inhabits the lovers' world; the lover as young boy runs upstairs after seeing *'Her eyes flash'* – but runs up to that lover's apartment of adulthood. In 'Eclipse' both mother and lover are united in a milieu of archaic gestures and symbols: ships at sea, candles at windows, Ariachne's line, the black bull and *'the steep galleries'*. Within this golden world of a personal, mythical vocabulary Theo Dorgan works out his unique Southern destiny as poet and citizen of the elect. It is part of the immortal charm of his mind, a teeming, crowded urban mind, that even as he embraces the object of his own desires he is conscious of, and concerned about, the below-stairs atmosphere. In the end it is important to honour his unique sensibility and awareness of others. More than any other Munster poet he is the one who answers the mid-century isolation and inert sexual maleness of Ó Ríordáin and Corkery. His world is an inclusive, attractive social world, for *'Downstairs/ the sailors are singing and at peace'*.

Seán Dunne,
Poet and Friend, 1956-1995

The poet and essayist Seán Dunne died in Cork City on the 3rd of August. His sudden death at the age of thirty-nine seems unreal, unjust and cruel. Even as I write these words I expect a phone call, explaining that it was all a mistake and that he had just gone away for a rest. Only yesterday, as I stood in Waterstones in Patrick Street, I thought I heard his beautifully resonant voice. But these are only the hallucinations of the recently bereaved. Seán Dunne is dead, and with him has gone a good deal of the energy and focus of literary Cork. The poets of the South needed his provocative presence, as well as his critical and anthologising energy.

But his death is first and foremost a personal tragedy. He is survived by three children, Gavin, Owen and Niamh, as well as his beloved Trish Edelstein and her son Merlin. Trish was with him when he died of a heart attack in his home at Kilcrea Park, near University College in Cork. It is Trish and the children as well as Seán's father, Richie, who must carry the real pain of loss. As Seán himself might observe, the poets can work out their loss in their own highly-subsidised, highly pampered good time.

Dunne was born in Waterford in 1956. He grew up in St John's Park, a bustling working class neighbourhood. During his childhood Waterford City was a busy and prosperous port, a town of thriving warehouses and glass factory. It was the home of Munster Champion hurlers and the mighty 'Blues' soccer team, the spawning ground of the Royal Showband and

Val Doonican. In his recent memoir *In My Father's House* (Anna Livia, 1991) he captures the flavour of that blue-collar world as well as the personal tragedy of his young mother's death.

Seán graduated from University College, Cork in 1976. His degree didn't mean much, other than that he had spent the previous few years in the vicinity of the University. He was immensely popular at College. Professors as well as undergraduates loved him, despite the fact that most of his seminars were held at The Long Valley bar. As the poet John Montague said at his funeral, "he was one of the brilliant students".

After graduating from UCC, Seán drifted between Waterford and Cork. He published a pamphlet *Lady in Stone* and was thrilled when he sold two copies to Leland Bardwell and Macdara Woods in a Dublin pub. After that he got a temporary job in Cork City Library where he survived for more than a year.

All the while he was writing poems, sending work out, getting published. In 1983 a group of his poems were published in *Raven Introductions 1*. In the same year he began to compile *Poets of Munster*, the first of his major local anthologies. In his Introduction he published an early Southern grumble against the poets of the North: 'They (Munster poets) come, in fact, from the wrong side of the tracks, though perhaps it would be more precise to say they come from the wrong side of the border. *Aquarius* is the only London journal to give them adequate space.' In later years he would modify that simple reading of the situation: indeed, his last essay, published in *Graph*, castigates the inflated reputations and notions of Southern poets.

His own early poems are precise and modest:

Stacked in jars on shelves, the beans
Diminish in time to favourite recipes.

('The Bean Feast')

These first poems were collected in *Against the Storm* (Dolmen Press). Ironically it was his admiration for two Ulster poets, Derek Mahon and Gerald Dawe, that led him into a new strategy for writing. The technical precision of Mahon's *Courtyards in Delft* shocked him out of easy ballad rhythms into colder and finer syllabic metre. Dawe's work on *Krino* as well as his critical writing taught Seán how to clarify poetic subject matter before proceeding with verse. By the time Dunne published *The Sheltered Nest* (Gallery, 1992) he had grown intellectually. But he had also discovered a myth, an enabling myth for his poetry: it was the myth of silence. His most recent works embody that new myth: 'I found that to live without such an inner silence seemed like an amputation of some vital part of myself.' In 1994 he published an account of that spiritual journey in *The Road to Silence* (New Island Books).

Seán Dunne's poetic journey was more brief than it should have been. Its brevity is a bitter injustice. But I have no doubt that he had already discovered an equilibrium, following the path of the poet Sean Ó Ríordáin who also journeyed away from the crowd and found a poetic silence among the Cistercians of Mount Melleray Abbey. As John Montague also observed at his funeral, "We have lost the poet but we have the poems."

A Poet Going Southward: Greg Delanty

In Cork City my own generation came to poetry under the shadow of two important deaths, the death of Ó Riada and Ó Ríordáin. The poetic laments of Sean Lucy, Montague and Kinsella for these dead heroes have left an indelible impression upon the heart of each of us. Seán Lucy's marvellous voice as he read from *Unfinished Sequence* and John Montague's insistent boom as he read from *A Slow Dance*: both seemed to create a map in the sand. They became the parameters of the Southern poem's possibility. The way to follow, the way a poet could show his or her basic education as well as the dutiful honouring of dead masters.

In the late Seventies and early Eighties it was difficult to remove oneself from our Southern primacy of elegy. Elegy is a compulsive atmosphere and young poets are particularly receptive to its powers. Around 1975–76, I could feel the heavy weight of bereavement that was shouldered from pub to pub. But this was the atmosphere out of which poems grew. Not to share in the atmosphere was to be excluded from the fertile earth of poems. But it was a consumptive earth as well, eating up the energy of creation in an orgy of remembrance. A poetic atmosphere that relies too heavily on grief and remembrance encourages conservative modes of thought. It is not life-giving in the sense that it is not interpersonal, not full of the give-and-take of sexual activity and late-night compromises. Elegy encourages an old poetry, not a young, critical, educated verse. But elegy was the atmosphere we knew best.

Ironically, at around the same time – while many of us were orientated towards consumption in the South and an early death for the sake of poetry – two poets emerged who were definitely not of the dying school. In fact, both poets were swimmers and life-savers, having both been teenage rivals at the Annual Lee Swim. I have a photograph from 1982 of the two poets, as they fled bare-bottomed after swimming naked at Innishannon House Hotel.

Buck-naked, they both looked like good poets. Neither looked patricularly marked by grief. Gerry Murphy was the first of these. He came back from the Israeli kibbutz in the late Seventies with a distinctively foreign poetry in his head – a poetry of Communist wars and conflicts, Fascists versus Republicans, Banana Companies against revolutionaries. No Irish poet since Charles Donnelly has described assassination so well, and only James Simmons of Ulster has described male lust with the same revolutionary irony:

> *the smooth delight*
> *of your breasts,*
> *the lovely slow curve*
> *of your hips, the southern tip*
> *of South America,*
> *that sort of thing.*

('A Small Fat Boy Walking Backwards'*)*

The second poet, athlete and life-saver Greg Delanty, is also an artist for whom the ocean brine has swept away the dank atmosphere of the distinguished dead. While a student at UCC Delanty worked summers as a life-guard on the Kerry beaches. Isolated from the atmosphere of John Montague's inner circle – the mourning circle – he developed a confident and distinctive personal style of poetry. In the last ten years he has done a spectacular backstroke against all the received styles of poetry, rising out of the Kerry water each September with a net-full of exquisite sonnets. In more recent times his personal style has been ventilated and affirmed by his sojourn in St Michael's College, Vermont, where he teaches poetry.

Delanty has retained the strength and grace of a good swimmer in his work. The easy conversational pace is the result of a great deal of energetic leg-work beneath the surface. He acquires and consumes poetic ideas at a rate faster than any other poet I know. He is curious, insatiable and energised with a very positive, sports-like competitive ease. For him poetry has been a learning process. In ten years he has used that diet of fitness and knowledge to make an extremely rare kind of literary personality: an Irish poet as much at home in Manhattan as Caherdaniel.

"Sometimes I think writers are sick creatures," says Greg Delanty. "The world doesn't exist until they write about it. It's through writing that they realise the world about them. And this was even more true for me when I first went to live in Vermont. At times, walking down the streets of Burlington, Ireland seemed so far away, so strange. I often doubted if Ireland still existed. I went to America on what I expected would be a short trip, but I stayed. Now I come home each summer only to find that Ireland is changing. Shops I used to walk into have disappeared and, of course, people die. That vanishing world threatens your sense of reality."

The poems in Delanty's book, *Southward*, published in Ireland by Dedalus Press, attempt to fix that changing reality. Delanty is the poet of our contemporary diaspora. He has been exiled from his native Cork city, but like many of the Ryanair generation he is too mobile to be defeated. He writes, in 'Home From Home',

> *Perhaps now I understand the meaning of home*
> *for I'm in a place, but it is not in me*
> *and could you zip me open you'd see*

between the break in fuming clouds,
an island shaped like a Viking's bearded head …

Two years ago, Delanty, Patricia, his American wife, and I were crossing Lake Champlain in a snow-storm. At one point the small ferry heading towards Vermont lurched violently, and our car was tilted forward. I gripped my seat, terrified. Delanty burst out laughing. I was reminded of that incident while talking to him about his new collection. I had just asked him the question: 'When are you satisfied that a poem is completed?" when my four-year-old son placed a large balloon at his left ear and threatened to burst it with a drawing pin. Delanty fell about in a fit of uncontrolled laughter. Soon the whole house was laughing. It is part of his great strength as an artist that he draws such incidents towards himself. He can make light of a tantrum and then go straight into the serious business of commentary. In the sequence, 'Myths', he writes, '*I didn't care how odd I looked\on the busy Saturday night street\ admiring you there outside Penneys.*'

But back to my initial question (before the balloon), to which he answered: "Once the poem is realised in the first draft there is always something flawed about it, something not quite correct. One has to clear away what is extra, to get at the original impetus or the place where the poem came from. It's like a sculptor with a block of stone, trying to get at the figure inside. You have the experience in you …. That's what you want to get at."

In conversation Delanty uses the word *realise* a great deal. For him poetry is not just a thing made, an artifact that exists coldly outside of the sphere of personal influences of the writer. The poem is intimately connected with the poet's life, with its personal origins. Each poem carries the implication that there is more than the mere text. In 'Thrust and Parry', for example, words are a kind of black magic. Yet he is very aware of the manufactured nature of lyrics. He uses a startling concentration of images, and equally startling combinations of metaphors. His poetry is a kind of Munster Martian:

> *Lazy, contented seagulls catch rides*
> *on the conveyer belt of a river*

or

> *Singing thrushes play on the fret board*
> *of electric wires.*

or

> *birds that CEILIDH – towards me.*

But the most powerful image in this new book is the early one of his father, the master-printer, who worked at the Eagle Printing Company in Cork. In 'Setting the Type' Delanty recreates the environment of the type-setting room. Like the American poet Roethke naming the rose-gatherers, Delanty names his father's workmates:

> *The names of Dan Hannigan, Owen Lane, Donnie*
> *Conroy –*
> *I could go on forever invoking the dead –*
> *were set deep in a boy*
>
> *impressed by the common raised type on the 3rd floor*
> *of Eagle Printing Company, 15 Oliver Plunkett Street,*
> *in the summer-still, ticking heart of Cork City.*

In 'The Master Printer' he describes the day he wore his first long pants. Again there is the presence of named others – he wonders if he will be noticed by Adolina Daly or Lily Walsh, his child-friends. Then there is the religious Brother who complains that the boy-poet is a bit slow. Delanty counters this early slight with a powerfully affirmative closure:

> *He did not know, blind behind a righteous frown,*
> *that you had the master-printer's skill*
> *of being able to read backwards & upside down.*

In poems like 'The Master Printer' he intuitively links his own world of feelings with the authority gained from his elders. The childhood peers of the early poems are gradually replaced by an equally populated adult world. Adolina and Lily are replaced by political friends from Simon, CND and People First.

Friendship is a key element in Delanty's life and work. He is the least secretive poet I know. For example, he has circulated the MSS of his collection among many friends and acquaintances, from his brother Norman to Christopher Ricks. He seeks out opinions and gets many people involved. He insists that this is part of his professional attitude to the writing. Yet the text of his poetry is terrifically populated.

Does he miss the companionship of Cork people; and does he miss that sense of isolation from the literary mainstream which is a common bond among Cork writers?

He was uncomfortable with the questions. "One has to be careful about laying down the line about our isolation and blaming it all on Cork. One is isolated as an artist anyway. I feel if you write the good poems, they'll come through in the end. For the writer, the writing is his home."

The Woman of the House

Having enjoyed the chauvinist snob Evelyn Waugh in the early 1980s, I hesitated before entering the minefield of Eavan Boland's *In Her Own Image*. Waugh was not a good starting point for the understanding of a unique voice in Irish women's writing; although it has to be said in Waugh's favour that his professional relationship with Nancy Mitford was full of mutual respect, the kind of respect that artists who understand completely each other's brilliance have for each other.

Eavan Boland had protested on a number of occasions that she didn't see herself as a feminist poet, but I knew from her broadcasts that she had suffered a feminist vision. She had discovered exclusive female experience as a value in itself. This wasn't a particularly original discovery in world terms, but it was a major breakthrough in Irish poetry. I remember bringing back from the University of Iowa in 1979 totally new books like Adrienne Rich's collections and Grace Paley's fiction. But the book that I most admired, for its supreme understatement and Dickinson-esque control of rage, was Jane Cooper's *Maps and Windows*. The centre-piece of that collection was a personal essay 'Nothing Has Gone into the Making of These Poems That Could Have Gone into the Making of Bread'. In the essay Cooper outlines her feeling of isolation and hopelessness as she watched the men in her family going off to war. (She comes from a distinguished family of aviators, her father having accompanied Lindberg to Ireland in the Thirties in a survey to find the most suitable site for an international airport). As a young woman Cooper felt that her duty was one of waiting, a kind of dutiful watchman of bad news.

Boland also has spent some of her young life waiting, except in her case she was waiting for the male aviators of Irish poetry to come to collect her. Her own early poems were traditional, male orientated, submitting to traditional themes and scholarly Irish sources. Derek Mahon in his essay on Boland's youth 'Young Eavan and Early Boland' in *Journalism* (Gallery Books, 1996) has this to say:

On reflection, I now realise that she was struggling to assert herself in what she correctly perceived to be a male-dominated literary culture. Was it, for her, a necessary struggle? She had only to look at a door and it flew open. But these were pre-feminist times, and Eavan wrote then, as she no longer does, for a notional male readership. She wanted to penetrate, indeed to dominate, the male oligarchy, but could, at that stage, do so only on their terms, or so she may have imagined.

In Her Own Image, I say without fear of contradiction, was the first serious attempt in Ireland to make a body of poems that arise from contemporary female consciousness. There was nothing in Boland's earlier books that helped one to unravel those new poems. All of the ten long poems that made this collection came out of the domestic micro-world of women, their body-consciousness, their baby-consciousness et cetera. Putting it in a literary way, one could say that Eavan Boland wasn't satisfied to go on looking at herself through the Muse-mirror of Kinsella. She chose to construct her own mirror that will allow her to say 'not renewable, but woman':

> *I look in the glass*
> *Myths are made*
> *by men.*

('Making Up')

Whether Boland believed that she was a feminist or not was irrelevant. She had written a collection that addressed itself to the feminist experience. Her poems therefore, were so new on the Irish scene that they pushed questions of excellence, correct construction, accepted modes of expression to one side. There was a triumphant affirmation of womanhood throughout the book that seemed to burst through old forms with confidence:

> then I begin to know
> that I am bright and original
> and that my light's my own

('Menses')

One couldn't read a book such as this without being infected by the value of its protest. To find raw female thoughts like these, one would have had to return to prose, to the stories of Kate Cruise O'Brien who also wrote out of an upper-class experience where the most intense female angers seem to fester.

In 1981 I told readers of *The Irish Times* that if they really wanted to get into Ms Boland's new book they could read it as part of a reading triangle with Kate Cruise O'Brien's *A Gift-Horse* and Adrienne Rich's book *Of Woman Born*. I wrote that it was more than a coincidence that some of the poems in *In Her Own Image* ('Mastectomy', 'Menses', 'Witching'), were dramatic monologues on subjects dealt with by Adrienne Rich.

In particular, Eavan Boland's poem on infanticide could have arisen from Rich's recollection of an evening spent with women poets (many of them mothers) in 1975, when they talked about a local woman who had murdered and decapitated her two youngest children. Rich recalled: "Every woman in that room who had children, every poet, could identify with her . . .

The words hate being spoken now, [yet] are being written down; the taboos are being broken, the masks of mother-hood are cracking through."

In this very carefully constructed book Boland attempted to speak with the voice of a disembodied female consciousness. In the early Eighties there was no model in Irish writing in English for the kind of leap that Boland made. Then we were unable to imagine the radical nature of feminism – very few commentators used the words that were adaquate: marginalisation, empowerment, inclusion. As for the sexuality of women, the integrity of their own sensuality as well as sensibility, there was just no awareness in our culture of the life energies that were frustrated.

One reads the pages of June Levine's *Sisters: The Personal Story of an Irish Feminist* with a feeling of chilled disbelief, yet the lines are totally honest and witnessed by thousands. Here is Levine's description of a Women's Liberation meeting:

Then Nell invited the audience to speak from the floor microphone provided. They queued up. At one stage I counted a line of fifty-two people. It was a moving experience. We had known those women were out there, but not so many, so willing to share their life's experiences and their views with us. It was spontaneous sisterhood, the Round Room a power-house of female energy. The sight of them brought me up in goose bumps, the sound of them the ultimate confirmation if we needed it that we Irishwomen needed liberation. It was the first time I'd been to a mass meeting run feminist style, everybody being given time to speak, and if someone was interrupted or cut off, a voice would come from the audience – a different one each time and not one of ours – 'let her speak, she's not finished yet.' The audience that night seemed to have an instinct for sisterhood ... They spoke off the cuff and were articulate and mostly to the point, like friends over a cup of coffee. Among other things, it was to be remembered as the night the first Irish unmarried mother declared herself publicly. I hadn't even *seen* one before and stretched my neck to get a better look at Helen Heaveny when she stepped up to the mike and said: 'I'm an unmarried mother ...' She had to pause while deafening applause encouraged her to go on. She spoke simply, practically, about having her child and rearing it on her own.

The invisibility of the unmarried mother, the fact that June Levine, a sophisticated woman, hadn't even *seen* one, is truly extraordinary, beyond belief in the 1990s. But it is a salutary admission: it reminds the complacent and those in contemporary denial about women's issues, about the true facts of the situation. It puts the radicalism of Boland's work into perspective.

In a more recent memoir, *Are You Somebody?* Nuala O'Faolain writes about the claustrophobia of the academic world and the cultivation of willing females as handmaids. Even a university education was no protection from the stereotypical usage of young women:

> I was soon commissioned to edit an anthology of Beckett criticism. This came about through being taken up by a very well-known English academic, who came to Dublin to give a lecture ... That was how it was, and perhaps is, when you are a young woman in a male-dominated field. The men dispensed patronage. They could tell you where the jobs were, and get you invited to conferences, and endorse you for grants, and mention your name to publishers. This wasn't exactly corrupt, but it wasn't fair, either; they wouldn't do it for you if they didn't like you ...

Which brings us back to the impulse and the material of *In Her Own Image*: within those pages Boland set down a new pattern for other women to follow. Coloured by the silence of emptied homes and the straying horses which seem to have escaped from the Parnassian halting-sites, her years in suburbia had cohered. Her *self* was centred. Gone was the Trinity seminar, the elaborate scaffolding of academic relationships, the Glass Kings of the male enterprise.

The Poet On His High Bicycle:

Austin Clarke and Our Free State Memory

A year ago, during the Spring Semester of 1995, I taught a course on Post-War Irish poetry to a group of twenty highly intelligent Americans. The use of the term Post-War was already a concession to my Minnesota hosts. When I'd planned the course I wanted to call it Poets of the Emergency and After. Having to explain the label would, I thought, expose the students to a kind of cultural centering within the indigenous Free State experience. The use of the word 'Emergency' is so locally Irish that it survives as an affront to contemporary Anglo-Irish commentary. It offends the notion now in vogue that the experiences of citizens of the Dáil, their memory of both oppression and national pride, offer only a narrow definition of Irishness, and a discredited one at that.

I'm aware that the use of the word 'Emergency' would marginalise me from many of the younger citizens of the Dáil itself. In truth, when I hear the word spoken now I think of my dead parents. I hear their voices from that 'twilight zone of time', as Conor Cruise O'Brien put it so beautifully in *Maria Cross*: 'that twilight zone of time which never quite belongs to the rest of history'. The impact of the word 'Emergency', like the words glimmer-man or illegal organisation, has begun to recede, just as the words knee-capping and proxy-bomb will recede as the experiences of our own generation grow dim and scatter.

Words and their political and cultural associations are important when one tries to reconstruct the full impact of a talent like Austin Clarke's. In order to know his work one must make a real effort to know his place and his time. His place is the Irish Republic, (a real country where people have created one kind of political culture) and his time is almost the entire span of years from the first banned book of the 1920s to the passing of the Divorce Referendum in 1995. The achievement of Clarke is that he has lived in our one place and cast a strong unerring eye upon the scene.

Which brings me back to the twenty young students in Minnesota, all poised, pen in hand, waiting to be informed. The course had just begun when one member of the class came to my office to complain. This young scholar had spent her Junior year at an Irish university. She was alarmed, she said, to find that I was going to spend three entire class periods on a poet called Austin Clarke. When she did Irish writing in Ireland, she was told that Clarke could be ignored.

I registered amazement at her Irish professors, these flawed cartographers of Irish verse

"Why didn't they teach him?" I asked.

"One said he was an old fart, that was how he put it," she explained. "All that Gaelic stuff as well. He wrote in Gaelic too, didn't he? They said it would bore non-Irish readers."

"I don't think it will bore you."

"He was anti-Catholic as well, wasn't he?" she asked dangerously. This is Minnesota, I thought, they hate bigotry as much as racism here.

"But he was a Catholic himself," I replied. "He wasn't bigoted, just angry. A lot of writers were very angry at that time. The Forties. The Fifties ..."

"Isn't Ireland very different now? Is it not a modern place full of young educated people?"

"It's not that liberal," I replied sheepishly.

When I had this encounter, the second Divorce Referendum was still eight months away. Perhaps this student had the gift of prophecy. She had created already a liberal and tolerant Republic. But I still carried within me the disappointment, even the rage, of Garret FitzGerald's failed referenda of the 1980s. The forces that broke Austin Clarke's heart were still at large, triumphant, arrogant, demented with moving statues and the faith of their fathers. I would not be mollified by the optimism of Summer Schools or the bland goodwill of our TDs. I gave Clarke his space because his life and work are beacons of intelligence that illuminate whole limping decades of Irish life.

In 1955 he had asked in 'Too Great a Vine' that vital question:

> *Fabulist, can an ill state*
> *Like ours, carry so great*
> *A Church upon its back?'*

I don't digress. What good is a poet if he or she cannot read the signs in a culture. Sure, there are signs and noises made by many different Irish poets; the noise of modernism made by Coffey and Devlin, the noise of political integrity made by MacNeice and Donnelly, the rich internationalism of Mahon and Muldoon, but none of these should exclude Austin Clarke, or would exclude him. He picked up the noises we made in our post-Independent Free State. He is the poet who embodies most courageously the struggle between the Catholic idea of public good and the fight for the autonomy of one's personal life.

"Don't skip those classes," I advised. "I bet you'll enjoy them."

And she didn't skip them. Indeed the same student contributed some of the liveliest insights into Clarke, especially later on when we discussed Máire Mhac an tSaoi and Nuala Ní Dhomhnaill. Ní Dhomhnaill's poem 'An Maidin sa Domhain Toir' with its harrowing lines:

Ní foláir ag teacht ag an saol so
go rabhas rochraosach; gur roghnaois
an bhullóg mhór is mallact mo mháthair
in ionad na bullóige bige is a beannacht ...

seemed to be a cry from a Martha Blake escaped from the massacre of Irish social life into the lonely domain of personal liberation. In that poem Ní Dhomhnaill had escaped from the oppressive place of haut-bourgeois mothers, abandoning the mere *usufruct* of bourgeois life for the freehold passion of her Anatolean lover. It is probably the key poem of my own generation, a woman's refusal to remain in *Éire*, secure but diminished. When outsiders think of the depravities of Irish life they automatically think of the ignorance of poverty, Irish Catholics in rags. In fact, the oppression of the soul can be as fierce for those who lived a very middle-class life. Young girls especially were restrained vigorously from engaging in any dangerous voyages of the psyche.

In 1937, at the age of forty-one, Austin Clarke returned to Ireland, or, more accurately, to the Free State, since Northern Ireland offered an entirely different public domain. By 1936 his *Collected Poems*, with a portrait of the poet by Estella Solomons, had been published. But despite this milestone he wasn't returning to a warm and receptive literary atmosphere. His novel, *The Bright Temptation*, had been banned four years earlier. Yeats had cruelly and inexplicably omitted him from *The Oxford Book of Modern Verse*. Indeed, Clarke's return from London to Dublin was like John Hewitt's return from Coventry to Belfast in later years. It's hardly surprising that the best review of Clarke's *Too Great a Vine* came from Hewitt, who understood only too well the nature of diminished homecomings. Almost simultaneously both poets would test their mettle against the public forces that oppress the spirit, Orangeism and Third Order Catholicism. Both forces were broad ethical masks for the narrow indigenous bourgeois interests running rampant and triumphant over the two Irelands.

In 1937, the most that Dublin could offer was the company of Denis Devlin and Donagh MacDonagh in the tea-room above the Green Cinema. A year later Clarke would be lampooned by Beckett (an artist who should have been his natural ally) in *Murphy*, and a year after that the outbreak of war would cut off his source of review income. Only broadcasts on Radio Éireann and work from R M Smyllie in *The Irish Times* kept the wolf from the door in the bleak years that followed.

Yet the period from 1937 to 1957 were, for Clarke, years of rigorous public engagement. Despite the tone of marginalised anger that one gets from some of the poetry, he was not a man to sulk quietly against the moral Gestapo that ran the Free State. As President of PEN (Dublin) he organised the Council of Action on Censorship in 1942. He founded the Lyric Theatre Company with Robert Farren in 1944. In 1949 he was at the funeral of President Hyde; in 1950 he attended the PEN Congress in Edinburgh. He appealed against the ban on *The Sun Dances at Easter* in 1952. A year later he attacked censorship in an article in *The New Statesman*. During this period of public endeavour he was also reviewing regularly, particularly for *The Irish Times*.

The sheer number of reviews he wrote is impressive. In the years 1954–56 he averaged nearly a review a week for *The Irish Times* literary page, sharing that influential space with luminaries such as Stephen Gwynn, Maura Laverty and Francis MacManus. He was a true professional, as reliable and consistent as Terence de Vere White or Dervla Murphy would be in later years. And he could review any author, any theme, from Wallace Stevens and F R Leavis to the more obvious Yeats (*Last Poems*, *Irish Times*, 14 February 1953) and MacNeice (*Autumn Sequel*, *Irish Times*, 24 December 1954). He had already reviewed MacNeice's *Autumn Journal* in *The Dublin Magazine* in 1941. In the mid-Forties he had also made what can only be seen as a prophetic statement about Ulster writing:

> The possibilities of an intensive literary movement in the North are exciting, and there are practical advantages which no serious author in this country can ignore. At the present time no enterprising publishing house can be established in Dublin owing to the restrictions of the literary censorship, and most of our writers, whether they wish it or not, are forced to publish in London or America. There is no reason why Belfast should not, during the next fifty years, become a publishing centre and an asylum for Irish writers.

If only he had lived to see the energy of the new Ulster Movement, the polemics and the poems, *The Honest Ulsterman*, and Blackstaff as well as Appletree and Lagan Press. Fifty years on, the energy he recognised in Robert Graecen's anthology comes properly into focus. But in the Forties and Fifties Austin Clarke's Dublin was frozen within a deep chill of censorship. Pamphlets of moral teaching dropped down upon the wastes of public life, ice to shrivel the heart. It was within this wasteland that Clarke the poet and brave observer, manouevred the fragile craft of poetry. The boatyard for his flotilla of small books was his own home. It was as if that scoundrel-time had withdrawn even the resources of the printing-press from any dissenting voice. In 1957, twenty-one years after his *Collected* had been published by Allen and Unwin and Macmillan (NY), Clarke was reduced to publishing *Too Great a Vine* in an edition of 200 copies.

What a world away this is from the best-selling poets of the Nineties. Yet this major poet was content to produce a booklet of twenty-nine pages – fifteen poems and two-and-a-half pages of notes. In his Notes of Occasions he wrote: 'As I have few personal interests left, I have concentrated on local notions and concerns which are of more importance than we are, keep us employed, and last long.'

But the first poem in this book concerns a matter of vital personal importance: the poet's house at Templeogue had been willed to the Archbishop of Dublin by Clarke's disapproving mother. He had been reduced to the status of a tenant on his own family property:

> *My mother wore no rural curch*
> *Yet left her savings to the Church,*
> *That she might aid me by-and-by,*
> *Somewhere beyond the threatening sky.'*

('Usufruct')

His satire is ferocious in these short poems. It has a personal, Swiftian fierceness. In the fourteen lyrics that surround the seventeen-stanza 'The Loss of Strength' he throws bricks at the passing clergy and councillors. The crippled, the trusting and the maimed, are listed by the poet in a kind of public flogging of the ravenous Church. In 'Miss Marnell', a portrait of a Catholic convert, we discover a willing servant of the Cause:

> *'False teeth got little acid from her food:*
> *But scribble helped to keep much mortar wet*
>
> *For convent, college, high institution,*
> *To build new churches or reduce their debt.*

The figure on the cross-cheque made restitution
For many sins ...

In 'Local Complainer' Clarke describes the dedication of yet
another garish Statue Of the Virgin:

Eight hundred pounds, cut, dressed and chiselled,
The best Italian marble. In welcome
The clergy came, the Mayor with gownsmen
Past derelicts of mill and warehouse
That bulge with emptiness ....

The mention of savings, cross-cheques and eight hundred
pounds gives his public commentary a bitter personal
resonance. Money is strength, especially in recession-hit
Ireland. A Church that drains so much hard cash from its
devoted followers is 'too great a vine' that turns the clay sour.
In the 1950s faith had a vibrant street-life. Clarke follows this
life around the Free State like a well-rehearsed heckler. In
'Pilgrimage' he sees sickness below and in the clouds, while in
'Marian Chimes' he endures the four-times-an-hour Mary
Immaculate bell:

So while we work, buy, sell,
Let habit in its cell
Mechanically hymn
Her praise, who pleads with Him
To aid us ...

Today we tend to think of the broadcast Angelus as
something timeless, immortally Catholic and Irish. The fact is
that the broadcast of the Angelus on national radio only came
about at the request of Archbishop MacQuaid in the early
Fifties. It is – like the sound of machine gun-fire on the Berlin

Wall – only a very specific local habit, developed at a restricted time.

The fourteen short poems in *Too Great a Vine* are a public cloak around the more private and meditative 'The Loss of Strength'. That loss of strength described in the poem was the result of a heart-attack suffered by the poet in the summer of 1955. The technical brilliance of this poem, with half-rhyme and internal rhyme as well as a rushing, interrupted rhythm, is an ironic tribute to the survival of artistic integrity at a time of great personal weakness. The poem follows the course of 'Farm brooks that come down to Rathfarnham' and all waterways whose energy is eventually forced beneath concrete paths and 'hidden in a tap'.

Maurice Harmon in his *Austin Clarke, A Critical Introduction* (1989) provides a comprehensive and incisive reading of this poem:

> In stanza after stanza he writes with mastery and ease. Having declared his acquaintance with the 'stone bed' of Ireland, a reference to the sleeping places of saints in the early Church, he moves in stanza five to a description of the journeys he made as a young man. That early self is recreated, his adventurous, optimistic quests re-enacted, with a slight touch of humorous self-mockery in the alliteratives of the opening line and in playful punning.

In 'Loss of Strength', Clarke the young poet of memory, takes to the hills on a bicycle of desire, away from the confined cell of the catechism:

> *Beclipped and confident of shank,*
> *I rode the plain with chain that freed me.*

What follows is a tour of imagined and sacred places. His wheel-rim turns through County Clare, across Medieval

Ireland, which was always his secure territory, where the old argument began between a primitive native Church and the Continental models of the post-Norman era. 'I saw God's light through ruins,' he says. It is part of his genius that he can juxtapose sex and engineering, scripture and terrors:

> *Monks, whom we praise now,*
> *Take down a castle, stone by stone,*
> *To make an abbey, restore the chain-light*
> *Of silence.*

The named ruins are an assembly of oppressive forces. Romanesque Ireland, Malachi of Bangor and Bernard of Clairvaux, are the assembled psychiatric notes left after the counselling session of the bicycle. The poet returns to the environment of Dublin Bay, to the capital of commerce and catechism, where he sees an Aer Lingus plane filled with pilgrims returning from Lourdes. He concludes:

> *The stream that wetted*
> *Forgotten wheels pushes past Rathfarnham,*
> *Half underground: slime step on stone.*
> *I count them – not my own.*

All of which brings me back to the beginning. To my student who was advised that Clarke could be ignored. What in injustice had been visited upon her. There is no doubt that some things in Clarke are irritating and raw. As Gus Martin pointed out in 1965:

> Part of the problem is that Mr Clarke has always existed on the fringe rather than the centre of society .... A sense of personal wrong has driven him to judge certain types of people – clerics, politicians – and their motives by

standards so harsh that they seem to contradict both the humanitarian and logician in him.

(*Studies*, 4, Vol LV, No. 216)

But what we lose when we avoid Clarke is the specific and lucid vocabulary of the profound moral crises in our culture. As well as the prosody, of course, as creative as anything in Pound's *Cantos*. I have yet to see a proper study of Clarke's prosody, described so well by Robert Farren as 'spring-water-music' in his *Course of Irish Verse in English* (1948).

Gus Martin was shrewd enough to see Clarke's influence on Donald Davie. One can also see the influence on Kinsella, Montague and Richard Murphy. To ignore Clarke is to teach badly. His voice is vibrant, astonishing and morally brave. When he unclipped his trouser-legs in 1955 and came into the ruined chapels, he donated more than an Irish sixpence to the less deceived world of English poetry.